TRUE CRIME CASE HISTORIES

VOLUME 5

JASON NEAL

AKAMAI PUBLISHING

Cover photos of:

John Famalaro (top-left)

Father Gerald Robinson (top-right)

Peter Madsen (bottom-left)

Carri Williams (bottom-right)

More books by Jason Neal

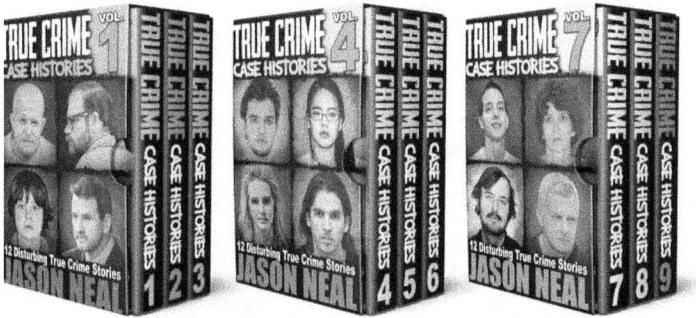

Looking for more?? I am constantly adding new volumes of True Crime Case Histories. The series **can be read in any order**, and all books are available in paperback, hardcover, and audiobook.

Check out the complete series at:

https://amazon.com/author/jason-neal

All Jason Neal books are also available in **AudioBook format at Audible.com.** Enjoy a **Free Audiobook** when you signup for a 30-Day trial using this link:

https://geni.us/AudibleTrueCrime

FREE BONUS EBOOK
FOR MY READERS

As my way of saying "Thank you" for downloading, I'm giving away a FREE True Crime e-book I think you'll enjoy.

https://TrueCrimeCaseHistories.com

Just click the link above to let me know where to send your free book!

CONTENTS

Introduction   ix

1. The Homeschoolers   1
2. The Submarine Case   15
3. Unlucky 13   27
4. Divine Justice   45
5. The Amish Killer   55
6. Cold Storage Killer   65
7. Coercive Control   77
8. The Werewolf Butcher   87
9. The Black Widow   99
10. The Crossbow Killer   107
11. Murder in the Sacristy   119
12. Devious Dixie   127
13. Bonus Chapter: The Broomstick Killer   141

Online Appendix   159
Also by Jason Neal   161
Free Bonus Book   163
Thank You!   165
About the Author   167

INTRODUCTION

Those of you familiar with my previous books in this series know that I always start off with a quick word of warning: real true crime isn't for everyone. Television shows and newspaper articles often gloss over the shocking details because it may be too grisly for the average viewer or reader.

When researching these stories, I commonly use actual police reports, court documents, and first-hand descriptions. Some of the details can be disconcerting. I do my best to not leave out any of the details in my books, no matter how depraved they may be. My intent is not to shock, but to show precisely how twisted the mind of a killer can be.

That being said, if you are overly squeamish, this may not be the book for you. If you're okay with it, then let's proceed.

Volume Five of True Crime Case Histories features twelve new stories taking place over the past fifty years. As with some of my prior books, I've focused on a few stories that happened near where I've lived or stories that I remembered being in the news as they were happening. With those stories, it wasn't until I had fully researched them that I realized how macabre they really were.

In this book, you'll read about a young, intelligent man that would rather kill his entire family with a crossbow than tell his girlfriend that he had been lying to her. You'll also read of the suburban housewife that endured thirty years of an abusive relationship before smashing her husband's skull with a hammer.

There's the story of the Amish man, tormented by the threat of Hell, that killed his wife because he thought she was the devil. There's also the Roman Catholic priest that ritualistically butchered a nun, stabbed an upside-down cross into her chest, and anointed her with her own blood.

Three stories in this volume take place in Washington State, one of which is of a young girl that ran away from her Seattle home in the 1970s. For thirty years, her parents believed she was a victim of Ted Bundy, until the real killer was finally caught. In another, a sexual sadist fancied himself a werewolf while he stalked and butchered his prey in unspeakable ways.

The stories in this volume are shocking and disturbing, but they're also true. These things really do happen in the world. We may never understand why killers do what they do, but at least we can be better informed.

I am constantly looking for new stories for future books and I prefer stories that can't already be found all over the Internet. Since the last volume, several of my readers have sent me murder stories that they remembered happening in their hometowns. In many of these cases, the stories had gone largely unreported other than the original reports in local newspapers - these stories are exactly what I'm looking for. If you remember a story that happened years ago, has been forgotten, and you'd like to see it written about, please send me any details you can remember and I will do my best to research them.

Lastly, please join my mailing list for discounts, updates, and a free book. You can sign up for that at

TrueCrimeCaseHistories.com

You can also purchase paperbacks, hardcovers, and signed copies of my books directly from me at:

JasonNealBooks.com

Additional photos, videos, and documents pertaining to the cases in this volume can be found on the accompanying web page:

https://TrueCrimeCaseHistories.com/vol5/

Thank you for reading. I sincerely hope you gain some insight from this volume of True Crime Case Histories.

- Jason

CHAPTER 1
THE HOMESCHOOLERS

I t's not clear what life was like for Hana Alemu in Ethiopia, but it's hard to imagine it could have been worse than it became when the eleven-year-old was adopted by the Williams family in Sedro-Woolley, Washington.

———

Larry and Carri already had seven children of their own and wanted more, but her last pregnancy had left Carri Williams unable to bear more children. It had become a trend for homeschooling evangelical Christians in the mid-2000s to adopt needy children into their already large families. The families felt that it was a duty of their faith to rescue children that needed a good home and then homeschool them according to a conservative Christian curriculum. Other families from their Bible study group had adopted as many as eight children into their lives; Carri and Larry wanted the same.

Larry Williams worked from noon until midnight as a mill-wright for Boeing, while Carri stayed home to homeschool their kids. Carri had attended a women's retreat run by a ministry called Above Rubies. During the retreat, they spoke of the trend among evangelicals to adopt children from Liberia, a west African country experiencing political insta-bility caused by multiple civil wars.

In 2008, the Williamses contacted Adoption Advocates International (AAI), a secular adoption agency based in Port Angeles, Washington. AAI was run by a woman named Merrily Ripley who had twenty children; three biological and seventeen adopted. Merrily informed Carri that there were two orphaned children in Ethiopia that needed a loving home. One child was deaf and Carri had studied American Sign Language before getting married, so it seemed like a perfect match.

To prepare for the adoption, the Williamses took a quick home-study course provided by AAI and filled out the neces-sary paperwork. AAI apparently missed the fact that Carri had left one section of the paperwork blank: the part about their beliefs on child discipline.

———

In the months leading up to the adoption, Carri and Larry saw a one-minute video clip of the children crying and begging for a good home. It was heart wrenching. Seven-year-old Immanuel was deaf and eleven-year-old Hana was slightly underweight at only 77 pounds.

Immanuel and Hana had been living in the Kidane Mehret orphanage in the Ethiopian capital city of Addis Abada. Both had been abandoned at an early age. Though they were not related, they were excited that they would soon become brother and sister living in the United States. Learning that their new parents lived in the idyllic countryside of the Pacific Northwest, Hana naively read *Little House on the Prairie* in preparation for her new, exciting life.

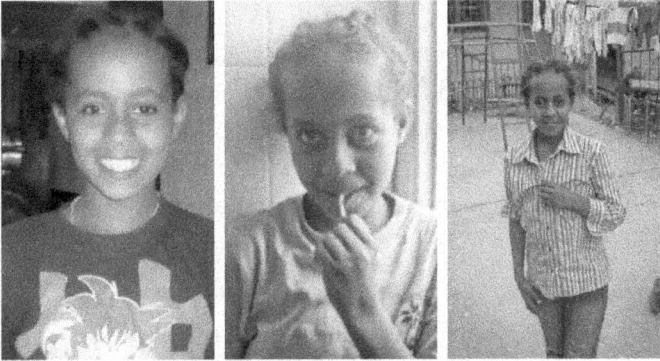

Hana Williams (Right photo in Ethiopia)

In the months after Hana and Immanuel's arrival in 2008, the Williams' post-adoption reports came to AAI as per the adoption agreement. According to the adoption agency, everything in the reports seemed normal and Hana had filled out to a healthier 105 pounds. However, in June 2009, the reports suddenly stopped. Although the adoption agreement stated that Carri and Larry would continue to send reports throughout the children's lives, technically they were under no legal obligation to file the reports. The adoption agency had no way of knowing the atrocities that were going on in the Williams household.

Larry and Carri Williams believed in a strict fundamentalist Christian lifestyle. In addition to homeschooling their children, almost all television and Internet access was prohibited. They believed women should never wear pants, only skirts or dresses and never swimsuits, and certainly never vote. The children were rarely seen in a public setting and only socialized with a select few like-minded families. Larry regularly preached to the children in the backyard of their rural five-acre property.

As for disciplining the children, the Williamses adhered to the teachings of a controversial book called *To Train Up A Child* by Michael and Debi Pearl. The book taught that the principles and techniques for training an animal and raising a child were the same. It instructed parents to begin spanking their children within the first few months of birth to "break their will."

In his book, Michael Pearl's argument for beating a child came straight from his interpretation of the Bible. Pearl believed that Proverbs 13:24 justified his beliefs:

> "He that spareth his rod hateth his son."

Pearl said,

> "A child properly and timely spanked is healed in the soul and restored to wholeness of spirit. A child can be turned back from the road to hell through proper spankings."

The book went into great detail of specific implements for parents to use; a wooden spoon, spatula, or the most popular weapon — a short length of small plastic plumbing tubing. This was a particularly well-liked implement because it could be easily curled up and kept available in a parent's pocket at all times. The book also taught parents to withhold food and put children under a cold outdoor garden hose as punishment.

The Pearls' book was extremely popular with fundamentalist Christian homeschoolers and, according to the author, sold almost 700,000 copies in the first seven years of its publication. The Pearls' No Greater Joy ministry generated upwards of $1.7 million tax-free dollars per year.

———

For the next two years, Hana's hopes of the American dream quickly washed away. Life with the Williams family was nothing like the *Little House on the Prairie* life she had envisioned.

Within months after Hana arrived in the United States, she began menstruating. This infuriated Carri, who told members of her knitting group that she had wanted to adopt "a little girl, not a half-grown woman." She complained that Hana was rebellious, telling her knitting friends, "I wouldn't wish her on anyone."

Friends and neighbors of the Williams family had noticed that Hana and Immanuel were often absent from public family outings, holidays, trips to town, or to church. On the rare occasion that they were brought to church with the family, one parishioner that knew sign language often attempted to sign with Immanuel, but Carri and Larry didn't want him communicating with anyone. One of them would quickly whisk the boy away before he had a chance to converse.

Neighbors noticed the seven children would be seen actively playing together at the front of the Williams' home, while Hana and Immanuel would be left standing alone near the driveway staring at their feet.

At home, the discipline was much worse than anyone could have imagined. Hana had Hepatitis B, which again infuriated Carri, who accused her of purposely smearing blood on the bathroom walls. Because of this, Hana was not allowed to use the bathroom in the house. She was only allowed to use a filthy outdoor portable toilet behind the barn that was only serviced twice a year.

The indoor shower was off limits too. Regardless of temperature, Hana's shower was a garden hose propped up with sticks in the front yard. Hana was often forced to use the cold makeshift shower while the other children watched from the windows of the warm house.

When Hana made any sort of complaint about the clothes that Carri had chosen for her to wear, she would lose her right to wear clothes at all, and given only a towel to wear for the day.

Hana had long braided hair that she was proud of. Her hair was the one thing she could take pride in and Carri knew it. The first spring of Hana's new life, she was told to cut the grass in the yard. When she finished, the grass was cut shorter than Carri had wanted it. As punishment, Carri shaved her head. She would later shave her head on two additional occasions.

The daily punishments had begun almost immediately after the children were adopted. Most of the time, Immanuel and Hana had no idea why they were being punished. It could have been for standing in the wrong place or getting an answer wrong on their schoolwork. They were never quite sure.

A few months after arriving in the United States, traumatized by the change of environment and daily punishments,

Immanuel began wetting the bed. Carri and Larry were convinced he was doing it on purpose just to anger them. The boy was taken outside and was given a shower with the cold hose, then sent to sleep in the dark shower room.

To add to his trauma, Carri often teased him by running the plastic tubing she called her "switch" up and down his face. On one occasion, Larry hit Immanuel on the top of the head with his fist and caused blood to run down his face. That night, he was made to sleep outside and the other children were told not to sign with him.

The punishments themselves were often straight from the *To Train Up A Child* book and involved beatings with a piece of plastic tubing that Carri kept in her bra. Sometimes it was one of Larry's belts folded in half, or a long, flexible piece of glue stick. Other common forms of punishment that the Williamses adhered to from the book included denying food, denying clothes, forced outdoor sleeping, and cold outdoor showers.

The Williams' biological children were punished, too, but never to the severity of Hana and Immanuel. The adopted children were fed different meals than the biological children. While the other children had sandwiches, Hana and Immanuel would have the same sandwich, but with a glass of water poured over it. Sometimes they would get cold leftovers with unheated frozen vegetables. Almost always, the two children were forced to eat outside while the other children ate inside, regardless of the cold, rain, or snow.

Because of Hana's menstruation, Larry and Carri took the initial steps to change her official age. Carri told her knitting group that if they could get her age bumped up a few years, they could kick her out of the house sooner when she turned eighteen. When another member of the knitting group asked how the girl would survive in the outside world, Carri snipped, "It wouldn't be my problem."

In the three years that Hana lived with the Williamses, she went from sleeping alone in the barn behind the house, to being locked inside a bathroom with no light, to eventually being kept in a four-foot by two-foot closet for up to twenty-four hours at a time. Larry's recorded bible sermons and religious music played outside of the closet the entire time, depriving her of sleep.

———

In the afternoon of Wednesday, May 11, 2011, Carri sent Hana into the backyard as one of her daily punishments. It was a rainy spring day and the temperature was in the mid-forties. When Hana, only wearing shorts and a t-shirt, complained that she was cold, Carri commanded that she do jumping jacks in the yard to stay warm. After a few hours alone outside, the children noticed Hana's lower lip quivering. She seemed unable to control her own movements, had fallen a few times, and eventually had trouble standing up at all.

Carrie went out the back door of the home and grabbed Hana by the arm and led her to the outhouse behind the barn. She continued to fall repeatedly, which infuriated Carri. She believed Hana was only trying to create attention. Unable to get her to stand, Carri left her lying alone in the yard.

Hours later, Hana's clothes were soaked. Carri set dry clothes on the back porch and yelled at her to come back inside the house. When Hana didn't return, Carri called on her two eldest sons. She gave the boys a length of plastic tubing and told them to hit her on her bottom for not following orders. Strangely, as the boys whipped her, she started to remove her own clothing and Carri called the boys back inside. By 5:00 P.M. Hana began throwing herself down on the pavement, gravel driveway, and grass. Her knees and hands began to bloody as Carri watched from inside the warm house. When she couldn't watch anymore, Carri turned away from the window and ignored Hana for the rest of the evening.

Near midnight, the seven biological Williams children giggled as they continued to stare out the window at Hana, who had removed all of her clothing and was still uncontrollably throwing her body around in a fit. She was wallowing in the mud and pounding her own head into the ground. They watched in amusement as Hana was experiencing what's known as "paradoxical undressing." In the final stages of hypothermia, the nerves can become damaged causing irrational behavior. This final stage of hypothermia tricks the mind into thinking it's extremely hot, causing the person to remove their clothes and attempt to burrow themselves into the ground.

When Hana finally stopped moving, one of the daughters called their mother to come check on Hana. She was face-down in the yard with a mouth full of mud. Carri, upset with Hana's nudity, grabbed a bedsheet and wrapped it around Hana. She then instructed her boys to drag her into the house.

First Carri called Larry, who was driving home from work. When she hung up, she finally dialed 911.

> "I think my daughter just killed herself.... She's really rebellious, and she's been outside, refusing to come in. And she's been throwing herself all around. And then she collapsed."

"Is she breathing?"

"I don't think so, no."

"How old is your daughter?"

"I don't know. We adopted her almost three years ago."

"You don't know how old she is?"

"She's somewhere between the ages of fourteen and sixteen. She was throwing herself all over the gravel, the yard, the patio. We went to bring her in. My sons tried to carry her in, and she took her clothes off. She's very passive-aggressive. I don't know how to describe it."

During the call, Carri sounded more annoyed than saddened or shocked. The 911 operator coached Carri through CPR, but it was no use. Hana was gone. When emergency crews arrived, Hana had a large lump on her forehead and she was covered in blood. Her hips, knees, elbows, and face had fresh red bloody markings from repeated whippings. She also had a stomach infection.

The postmortem examination of Hana's body revealed she was abnormally thin for just thirteen years old. At only five feet tall, she was emaciated and had gone back down to 76 pounds. She was lighter than 97% of girls her age and thinner than she was when she originally came from Ethiopia three years earlier. The official cause of death was hypothermia compounded by malnutrition and gastritis (stomach infection). It was determined that her body had been too thin to retain enough heat on the day she died.

———

When Child Protective Services knocked on the door of the Williams home the following day, Larry refused to let them in. Two weeks after Hana's death, the entire family were interviewed by detectives and Child Protective Services. All the children gave the same story, obviously coached by their parents: Hana was rebellious and "possessed by demons."

When Immanuel was interviewed, he told detectives, "People like Hana got spankings for lying and go into the fires of Hell." When Larry heard Immanuel give that answer, he immediately stopped the interview and took the children home.

Two months had gone by with no charges brought against the Williamses when Child Protective Services received an anonymous tip. Someone claimed that Carri didn't like her adopted children and Immanuel was being treated much like Hana. With that news, CPS worked with detectives and opened a formal investigation. All eight of the Williams children were taken into foster care. During a search of the house, police found a copy of the book *To Train Up a Child*.

Even after months in foster care, Immanuel was afraid of his foster parents and nervously apologized for every little mistake he made, even asking his foster mother why she wasn't beating him. He told his therapists of repeated nightmares and constantly worried that he would be the next to die. Immanuel was diagnosed with post-traumatic stress disorder.

That September, more than four months after Hana's death, Carri and Larry Williams were arrested on charges of homicide by abuse and first-degree manslaughter for the death of Hana, as well as first-degree assault of a child for the abuse of Immanuel.

Carri and Larry each faced a potential life sentence. Both posted bail of $150,000 each, but were given strict orders to not contact each other or any of their children — either directly or through third parties or other means. However, when Larry continued to send highlighted bible verses to the children, the prosecution believed them to be coded messages encouraging them to come to his defense. Larry Williams was arrested again and placed in a state jail where he remained for almost two years awaiting trial.

———

This wasn't the first time that the book by Michael and Debi Pearl, *To Train Up a Child*, had been linked to a child's death. Two other sets of fundamental Christian parents that employed tactics from the book had recently killed their adopted children: Sean Paddock and Lydia Schatz. The three deaths happened in different parts of the United States, but all were adopted, homeschooled, and beaten with a length of 1/4 inch plastic tubing, as recommended by Michael Pearl.

Seven-year-old Lydia Schatz's parents, Kevin and Elizabeth, held her down and beat her for nine hours with a piece of the tubing for pronouncing the word "pulled" incorrectly. Four-year-old Sean Paddock's mother Lynn Paddock smothered him in a blanket wrapped too tightly around him because she wanted to stop him from getting out of bed in the middle of the night. Like Hana, the abuse that eventually killed these children was just the tip of the iceberg.

———

At trial, Carri and Larry turned on each other. The couple sat at opposite tables in the courtroom, rarely looking each other in the eye. Larry testified that the discipline was all at the hands of Carri, while Carri testified that her discipline was at the instruction of her husband. Carri also admitted that she told her children not to talk to detectives about any of the abuse. The children, however, testified that lying was considered one of the most serious offenses in their household.

One of the Williams children, Joshua, confirmed that Hana had not been homeschooled or eaten meals with the other children for at least a year before her death. The child told the court that she would sometimes go two days without anyone speaking to her and none of the biological children liked her, "but it didn't matter because she was always in the closet."

Immanuel testified using sign language with the help of three interpreters. The courtroom was silent as he was asked what he thought happened to Hana. "I don't know" he signed. "She disappeared. I think maybe she's dead." He also testified that he was often beaten with a stick or plastic tubing until blood ran down his face, telling the court, "I would suffer with the pain until it eventually went away."

The biological children admitted that they were coached to tell authorities that Hana slept in the bedroom with them, when in fact she slept in a tiny locked closet. The jury was shown the closet that she slept in and were shown photos of the scars on Hana's body from repeated beatings.

Larry testified that he trusted his wife's discipline choices with the adopted children because she had done such a good job raising the other children. Carri rebutted that her husband was an equal participant in the discipline and even came up with some methods on his own, like hosing off Immanuel and locking him in the shower room after his bedwetting. She also testified that Larry was the one that installed the lock on the closet door.

During the trial, the defense attempted to argue that Hana was actually sixteen-years old rather than thirteen. If she had been sixteen at the time of her death, the homicide-by-abuse charge could not be applied as it only applies to children younger than sixteen.

Since there was no documentation of her birth from Ethiopia that proved her age either way, the trial was postponed to have Hana's body exhumed for examination. Tests on her teeth and bones, however, were inconclusive and experts couldn't confirm that she was sixteen.

The defense agreed that Larry and Carri may have been bad parents and their choices were bad, but they weren't killers and had no idea that their form of discipline would lead to the child's death.

After seven weeks of testimony, the jury didn't agree with the defense and both Larry and Carri Williams were convicted of first-degree manslaughter and first-degree assault. Carri was also found guilty of homicide by abuse and was sentenced to thirty-seven years in prison. Larry Williams was sentenced to nearly twenty-eight years and given credit for the almost two years he had been in jail awaiting trial.

CHAPTER 2
THE SUBMARINE CASE

For more than 100 years, Refshaleøen - a large industrial area in the port of Copenhagen, Denmark - was home to Burmeister & Wain, one of the world's leading diesel engine producers for large ships. The company thrived for 150 years, employing over 8,000 people until the global competitiveness of the shipping industry in the 1970s eventually caused the company to collapse.

Over 120 acres of dilapidated shipyard sat abandoned for the next decade or so. By the late 90s, the warehouses, with their rusted metal landscapes and cheap rents, became home to local aspiring artists and entrepreneurs.

The artificial island was only a quick ten-minute bike ride from the city center of Copenhagen. By the late 2010s, the area had grown into a vibrant, thriving hipster bastion. Over time, the starving artists were eventually pushed out by flourishing tech firms, craft breweries, and food vendors. Today, the area features many popular restaurants including Alchemist. Consistently rated one of the best restaurants in the world, it features $15 million decor and seats only forty guests for a five-hour meal at $700 a plate. The area is also home to the annual Copenhell heavy metal festival, featuring some of the largest names in heavy metal such as Ozzy Osbourne, Tool, KISS, and Iron Maiden.

One of the better-known entrepreneurs that had occupied the area was Peter Madsen, a Danish inventor, artist, and entrepreneur known to many as "Rocket Madsen." He was an eccentric, self-taught aerospace engineer who had built three submarines, several rockets, delivered a popular Ted Talk, and was working on a personal rocket designed for human travel in 2017 that he described as an, "intercontinental ballistic missile passenger ship." He was known as a charismatic dreamer that some thought of as an aspiring, small-scale Elon Musk or Richard Branson.

Peter Madsen / Kim Wall

———

Kim Wall was an independent journalist living in Copenhagen and thought Peter Madsen would be an excellent subject for one of her long-form articles.

Kim was exceedingly intelligent and eternally curious. To hear her friends describe the petite redhead as "a badass" was a gross understatement. The ambitious thirty-year-old had written many articles that had taken her all over the world.

Born and raised in Sweden, Kim spent most of her adult life scouring the globe. She earned her bachelor's degree in international relations at the London School of Economics, then moved on to graduate with honors from Columbia University in New York with two master's degrees in journalism and international relations.

Kim's writings were certainly not fluff pieces. She wrote articles on foreign policy, social justice, climate change, nuclear weapons testing, gender, and pop-culture. Her stories took her all over the world, to places like Sri Lanka, North Korea, India, Australia, Haiti, Cuba, and Uganda. She believed that the best stories were not told from inside a newsroom; she needed to be in on the action. Her extensive client list included The New York Times, Harper's, BBC, The Guardian, Time, The Atlantic, Vice Magazine, Slate, The South China Post, and many others.

On the evening of August 10, 2017, Kim and her boyfriend Ole Stobbe were preparing to host their going-away party. In six days, they were planning to move from their home in Copenhagen to Beijing, China.

At 5:00 P.M. that evening, Kim received a text message from Peter Madsen inviting her to his nearby workshop for tea. She had been trying to get an interview with him for several weeks. If she wanted to get that interview before she left for Beijing, this was her last chance. She agreed and left for his nearby hangar warehouse.

Just thirty minutes later, Kim came back home. She grabbed a few things and told Ole she was going for a two-hour ride with Madsen on his Nautilus submarine and would have to miss the first few hours of their going-away party. The UC3 Nautilus was a fifty-eight-foot midget submarine that Madsen had designed and built himself.

Madsen told Kim that they could take a quick trip around the bay surrounding Copenhagen and she could interview him during the trip. She could even make it back for the last few hours of their party.

That Thursday evening, Kim left for the pier not far from their apartment where Madsen's submarine was docked. Just before 7:00 P.M., she texted Ole a photo of the Nautilus with the message, "I'm still alive btw [by the way]." As they cruised through the bay with the tower still above the water, she sent him another photo of nearby windmills. Moments later, as Ole was entertaining their guests at the waterside barbecue, he and their friends saw Kim waving from the tower of the submarine. Kim sent a final text to Ole, "Going down now! I love you!!!!!!" That was the last time they would see Kim alive.

———

For several weeks in 2017, an Australian filmmaker, Emma Sullivan, had been filming a documentary about Madsen and his group of engineers for Sky News. That evening, neither Sullivan nor Madsen's assistants had known anything about his meeting with Kim Wall. This seemed strange at the time, considering the close proximity they had all been in during the filming. However, in hindsight, it became clear that Madsen had purposely hidden the existence of Kim because he knew what was to come.

Kim should have returned by 10:00 P.M. that night, but there was no word from her and no sign of the submarine at the pier. The goodbye party had moved from the waterfront to a nearby bar, but when Ole returned home late that night and Kim was still not back, he was worried sick. Ole rode his bike around the island, searching for her in the dark, but found nothing. Frustrated and frightened, Ole called police just before 2:00 A.M. to report his girlfriend missing.

Peter Madsen & Kim Wall aboard the UC3 Nautilus Submarine

By dawn, the Danish Navy had issued a full-scale maritime search using two helicopters, three ships, and several private boats. There had been no distress calls issued the prior night. Finally, several hours later, the Nautilus submarine was spotted floating in the bay south of Copenhagen.

Witnesses on nearby rescue boats saw Madsen in the submarine's tower wearing his trademark military fatigues. He then disappeared inside the tower for a moment and a loud "whoosh" of air was heard coming from the sub. Seconds later, the submarine quickly started to sink and Madsen climbed out. It only took about thirty seconds for the sub to sink as he swam toward the nearby boats.

Madsen was rescued unharmed from the sinking vessel. But the question remained… where was Kim? Rescue boats brought him back to Copenhagen and dropped him at the dock. Television crews filmed him giving a thumbs-up as he stepped off the boat. Madsen told the waiting cameras,

> "I couldn't close any hatches or anything. But I guess that was pretty good because otherwise I still would have been down there."

There was no mention of Kim.

Police detained Madsen for questioning, but when he was asked of Kim's whereabouts, he looked confused. According to Madsen, he had dropped Kim off at the same pier that he had picked her up from. He said the two of them went on a quick cruise of the bay before he dropped her off, as planned, and decided to go back out in the submarine by himself.

The police didn't believe Madsen's overly vague story and suspected that he had intentionally sunk the submarine in an attempt to destroy evidence. He was arrested for preliminary involuntary manslaughter,

> "for having killed in an unknown way and in an unknown place Kim Isabel Fredrika Wall of Sweden sometime after Thursday 5:00 P.M."

That Saturday, Madsen was brought into a closed-door court session. When asked again about Kim, he changed his story. Madsen admitted that he lied when he said he had dropped her off at the pier. He then claimed that he was holding the submarine hatch open for her when he lost his footing and his hand slipped. The hatch fell on her head, crushing her skull and killing her instantly. He told authorities that he had panicked, pulled her body out of the hatch, and "buried her at sea."

If Madsen's story was true, police would know soon enough. Kim's body was bound to wash up ashore sooner or later, so police continued their search of the bay.

On August 21, eleven days after Kim went missing, a cyclist riding along the shoreline of Amager Island noticed something that had washed up on the shore. Upon closer inspection, the cyclist could tell it was part of a human body. It was a torso, missing the arms, legs, and head.

Using DNA from Kim's hairbrush and toothbrush, the torso was positively identified as that of Kim Wall. She had been stabbed fifteen times—fourteen of which were in and around her vagina. It was obvious that Kim's death was no accident. Prosecutors changed their charge against Madsen from involuntary manslaughter to murder and improper handling of a corpse.

Divers searched the area where the torso had been found and where the submarine had gone down. Over the course of the next month, Kim's head was located, as were both of her legs. All three were in bags with large pieces of metal to help weigh them down. They also found her orange fleece sweater, shoes, socks, and black and white skirt, along with a knife. All were packed inside another plastic bag with large pieces of lead.

Medical examiners found no fractures or wounds on Kim's skull, ruling out the possibility of her being struck on the head by the submarine hatch. It was determined that the likely cause of death was strangulation.

Despite the discovery of the dismembered body and no damage to her skull, Peter Madsen still insisted Kim had died from an accidental hit on the head. He had no explanation for the dismemberment or stab wounds.

———

Madsen sat in jail while detectives learned more about him and his strange proclivities. Although he was seemingly happily married, Madsen enjoyed his sexual freedom and was known for experimenting in various fetish groups.

When forensic detectives searched Madsen's computer and iPhone, they found over 140 video clips, many of which were "snuff films." Madsen had a morbid fascination of videos featuring simulated, animated, and actual death. The videos depicted women being beaten, strangled, and tortured. There were also videos of decapitation. His browser search history showed that he has searched the Internet for "beheadings" just before their ride in the submarine.

Madsen denied that any of the videos on the computer were his. He told investigators that the computers were often used by his office staff and an intern; he claimed that the videos could easily have belonged to any one of them.

When detectives interviewed Emma Sullivan, who had been filming the documentary about Madsen, she told them that in an interview just days prior to Kim's death, Madsen mentioned that he was, "worried that he might be a psychopath." He also spoke to her about his fixation of having sex on a submarine.

As the prosecution built their case against him, Madsen changed his story yet again. This time he claimed that Kim had died of accidental carbon monoxide poisoning while she was inside the sub and he was up on the deck. This new explanation was his excuse for why there was no damage to her skull. His theory was later shut down by the Danish Navy after their examination of the submarine showed no traces of carbon monoxide or CO_2.

Madsen also admitted to dismembering her and dumping the body parts in the sea. The charges against him were changed once again to murder, indecent handling of a corpse, and sexual assault without intercourse.

At trial the next January, Madsen entered a plea of not guilty. The prosecution read aloud a casual text that he wrote to his wife just moments after he killed Kim Wall.

> "I am on a little adventure with Nautilus, sailing at sea by the moon, I am not diving. Kisses & hugs to the kittens."

The prosecutor queried Madsen on how he had the composure to send such a casual text after such a traumatic event on the submarine. Madsen replied:

> "I know that my wife would worry. I couldn't think of much else than that there was a catastrophe on the submarine."

When asked why he decided to dismember and dump Kim's body if it was all just a tragic accident, Madsen said that he suffered a temporary "psychosis." He claimed that he dismembered her to,

> "..save her family. It's something so horrible that I do not want to go into detail."

The prosecution pushed him to elaborate and Madsen told the court that it was an unbelievably insane situation which made him think of the movie Se7en, when Brad Pitt found his wife's dismembered head in a box at the end.

Eventually Madsen went into detail about the killing and how he needed to put Kim's legs into the toilet to stabilize her body as he sawed off her head. Madsen claimed,

"…it was very unpleasant and not planned."

He continued, explaining that he used a nineteen-inch sharpened screwdriver to puncture her body.

"Yes, I put some punctures in the body parts because I didn't want them to be inflated by gases. There's nothing sexual in the fact that the stab wounds were in and near her vagina. I understand why you might want to think there was, but there was nothing sexual in it for me."

Even the defense's witnesses couldn't deny his obsession with snuff films, murder, and where to hide body parts. A former "mistress" explained that he belonged to various sexual fetish clubs and had confided to her his "ideal murder" fantasy. This involved filming the murder of a woman while he and friends dismembered the body together.

She also recalled that he was kicked out of a BDSM (Bondage & Discipline / Domination & Submission / Sadism & Masochism) club for being overly creepy,

"not because he was too extreme, but because he was too passive. He seemed fascinated, but not turned on."

One witness told the court about a video that Madsen once showed her of a woman being strangled with a wire. Yet another witness testified that he had said Koge Bay would be,

"a good place to dump a body because it was a busy shipping area and it would be difficult to use sonar."

The jury also heard testimony from psychiatrists that had questioned Madsen during his incarceration. During his sessions, he spoke of the dismemberment of Kim's body with no emotion.

> "What do you do when you have a big problem? You divide it into something smaller. A dead body does not deserve any special respect."

The psychiatrists agreed that Madsen had narcissistic and psychopathic traits, adding that he had,

> "a severe lack of empathy and remorse" and described him as, "extremely untrustworthy and a pathological liar."

Another witness testified that Madsen had repeatedly invited her onto the sub just two days before killing Kim. The prosecution used this information to help establish premeditation; they argued that Madsen had been actively trying to lure women to the submarine.

The prosecution also argued that Madsen showed premeditation when he brought along tools such as a nineteen-inch sharpened screwdriver and saws — tools that typically aren't needed on a submarine.

When the prosecution asked Madsen of his childhood, one of his answers was particularly bizarre: "I wanted to be a victim in a child porn film."

On March 8, 2018, Peter Madsen was found guilty of murder, indecent handling of a corpse, and sexual assault. He was sentenced to life in prison.

———

While in prison, on December 19, 2019, Madsen married Jenny Curpen, an eccentric Russian artist living in exile in Finland. Initially Curpen announced the marriage was part of an "art project" called "This is not the Peter we knew." She later claimed the marriage was genuine.

Emma Sullivan's documentary about Madsen, "Into the Deep," premiered at the Sundance Film Festival and was originally slated for an April 2020 release on Netflix, but the deal with Netflix has since been withdrawn.

CHAPTER 3
UNLUCKY 13

I t was a rainy Friday afternoon, April 13, 2012, when Brittany Killgore-Wrest began packing her bags. Brittany's online profile name was "13smyluckynumber," but this Friday the 13th was going to be anything but lucky.

Just three days earlier she had filed for divorce from her husband, Lance Corporal Cory Killgore. Cory had been a Marine stationed at Camp Pendleton just north of San Diego, but had recently been transferred for a tour of duty in Afghanistan, leaving Brittany alone in the small military town of Fallbrook, California.

As a teenager, Brittany had dreamed of marriage and wrote about it on her blog:

> "I want to be married. I want to love that person. But the divorce rate is so high."

She also wrote candidly of her insecurities and struggles with depression. Three years later she was married, but the marriage wasn't what she had hoped it would be. Both Brittany and Cory were only twenty when they married, but by the time they were twenty-two they mutually called it quits.

Brittany Killgore

Fallbrook was a small town that sat immediately east of the entrance to U.S. Marine Corps' Base Camp Pendleton. With a population of just 30,000 people, most of the town was comprised of military families. Brittany lived at the La Galiana de Cortez apartments in a small upstairs apartment just a short walk from the entrance to the base.

She had grown up in The Ozarks in Missouri, but her family had since moved to Pennsylvania. Once her divorce was finalized, she would have no reason to stay in the military town, so on that rainy afternoon she and her friend Channy Tal were packing boxes for her move to Pennsylvania.

———

That same afternoon, another of Brittany's friends, Elizabeth Hernandez, had stopped by the home of Dorothy Maraglino and Louis Perez to return a camera charger she had borrowed. In casual conversation, Elizabeth mentioned that her friend Brittany was moving away from Fallbrook. She told Dorothy that she was planning to take her to the marina in San Diego and treat her to a Hornblower dinner cruise before she left.

Dorothy was familiar with Brittany. In fact, she had a deep hatred of the girl. Although she barely knew her, Dorothy often called Brittany "the disease" or "the herpes."

Dorothy was in a polygamous open relationship with U.S. Marine Staff Sergeant Louis Perez, a sixteen-year veteran of the 3rd Marine Aircraft Wing stationed at Camp Pendleton. The couple had agreed that they were free to see other people, but despite the open relationship, Dorothy felt threatened by Brittany Killgore. Brittany was young and beautiful; Dorothy believed she was too flirty with forty-five-year-old Perez. She often asked Elizabeth why she hung out with Brittany at all and once jokingly told her, "I could get rid of her for you."

Dorothy Maraglino and Louis Perez's relationship was far from normal. The fact that their relationship was polyga-mous, however, may have seemed like the most "normal" part of the relationship. The two lived as "Master" and "Slave" in a twisted BDSM (Bondage & Discipline / Domina-tion & Submission / Sadism & Masochism) relationship.

For years, Perez lived as the dominant (Master) of the house-hold, while Dorothy lived as the submissive (Slave). Dorothy was also a "switch," meaning she was submissive to Perez, but would also be a dominant (Mistress) to her own slaves.

Together, the two of them took part in their BDSM lifestyle with their live-in slave Jessica Lopez.

Each participant in the three-way relationship had their respective BDSM names; Louis Perez was "Ivan," Dorothy Maraglino was "Dee," and Jessica Lopez was "Rosalin."

Within the household, Dorothy established strict written rules including the "House Manual," "Perfect Slave Checklist," and a "Slave Contract." Dorothy (Dee) also had a contract that professed her as the sole property of Perez (Ivan). The contract, entitled "Deed to Dee," was signed in Dorothy's bloody thumbprint. The vanity license plate on Dorothy's truck read, "IVNS KTN" (Ivan's Kitten).

Dorothy Maraglino controlled everything that Jessica Lopez (Rosalin) did in life—both inside the home and out. Jessica wore a red dog collar at all times with a heart-shaped dog tag engraved with the text "Rosalin - Property of Ms. Dee" and ate her meals out of a dog bowl. Louis, however, as Dee's master, had control over both Dorothy and Jessica.

Louis Perez was a sadist. He lived to inflict pain on others. In prior relationships, he had choked his partner every time they had sex, either with his hands or with a leather belt. Occasionally he suggested having his slaves kidnapped by strangers, held prisoner, and tortured. Knives and chains were common sex toys in his relationships. Perez kept videos of himself beating women as they begged him to stop. One such video showed him beating a woman into unconsciousness.

On another occasion, Perez and Dorothy acted out an abduction fantasy where they picked up a young woman in a parking lot and took her to their "dungeon" in the basement of Dorothy's home for BDSM "play."

———

Later that rainy Friday at 4:38 P.M., Louis Perez knocked on the door of Brittany's apartment as she and Channy were packing boxes. It surprised Brittany to see him, considering she barely knew him, and she asked how he knew where she lived. He replied, "I asked around."

Perez explained that he had purchased two tickets for a Hornblower dinner cruise later that night and wanted to know if she'd like to go with him. It was an odd request, considering they weren't close friends. There was a twenty-three-year age difference and she knew he was in a relationship. Brittany was noticeably uneasy about the proposition and politely declined his offer, explaining that she needed to pack boxes for her move. Perez wrote down his phone number and handed it to her: "Call me if you change your mind."

When Perez left the apartment complex, he sent a text to Dorothy reading, "That wasn't successful." She replied, "Tomorrow is another day."

Just minutes later, Perez got a text message from Brittany. She wanted to know if he knew anyone that could help her with her move. Perez was quick to reply, "Party with me tonight & you'll have five guys there in the morning."

Still uncomfortable, Brittany messaged him saying that she would love having help with her move, but felt weird partying with him because she knew he was in a relationship with Dorothy. He replied, "She's ok with it, here's her phone number. Give her a call."

Brittany sent a brief text to Dorothy who immediately called her back. On speakerphone, Brittany's friend Channy heard the conversation. Dorothy encouraged her to go on the dinner cruise with Perez. She told her they'd already paid for the tickets and explained that, as she was pregnant with Perez's baby, being on a boat would probably make her seasick anyway.

After hanging up with Dorothy, Brittany told Channy that she still didn't feel entirely comfortable with it and had no interest in Perez romantically, but really liked the idea of champagne and a three-course-meal sailing on a yacht beneath the Coronado Bay Bridge.

By 6:10 P.M., Brittany had changed her mind. She sent a text to Perez agreeing to go with him, to which he quickly responded, "Be ready at 7:30."

What Brittany didn't know was that the Hornblower dinner cruise left the dock at 7:00 P.M. - and the dock was an hour away from Fallbrook. There was no chance they would make it. But that didn't matter… Perez never had tickets, nor any intention on taking her on the cruise. He had other plans.

———

Brittany borrowed two evening dresses from Channy for the dinner cruise and decided on a dark purple one with a glittery purple flower pattern. Still feeling awkward about the situation, she gave Channy the cell phone numbers of both Perez and Dorothy. Just in case.

At 6:38 P.M., Brittany messaged Elizabeth Hernandez to let her know about her date with Perez. Elizabeth was confused; she had planned on being the one to take Brittany on the dinner cruise as a gift. She had even mentioned her intentions to Perez and Dorothy earlier in the day. She also thought it was strange because she knew that Brittany barely knew Perez.

Brittany received a text at 7:31 P.M. from Perez, "I'm running late, be there in five minutes. Can you meet me at the curb?"

Brittany replied, "At the curb? It's raining, you know. I'd appreciate it if you drove into the complex."

"It's not. I don't want to miss our boat," Perez responded.

He knew there were security cameras throughout the complex and wanted to avoid them, but drove through anyway. At 7:36 P.M., surveillance cameras showed his white Ford Explorer entering the complex. One minute later he texted, "I'm here."

At 7:39 P.M. Brittany messaged another friend, Jessica Perry, that lived in her same apartment complex:

> "I'm going on a dinner cruise with Louis Perez tonight. I might stop by to see you when I get back."

One minute later, the apartment security cameras showed the Explorer leaving the apartment complex with Brittany in the passenger seat.

Just ten minutes after Brittany left the apartment complex, Channy received a one-word text message from Brittany's phone. It simply read, "Help."

At approximately the same time, Perez messaged Dorothy: "Kitten?"

———

The message gave Channy Tal a sudden twinge of fright. She immediately replied to Brittany, "What? R U okay?" There was no reply, so she messaged again, "Brittany are U okay? I am freaking out here." Still no reply. Channy messaged one more time before she finally got a reply at 8:05 P.M., "Yes, I love this party."

Channy knew the reply was not genuine. Brittany would never have used the word "Yes" in a text message - she had always just used "Yeah."

After trying to call Brittany several times with no answer, Channy sent another message demanding her to call back, "Call me back now! I need to hear your voice."

At 8:07 P.M., Channy received another text, "In a few. hot guys." Channy was certain this wasn't Brittany and insisted that she call her immediately. At 8:09 and 8:10, Channy received two short phone calls. Both calls were only a few seconds long with loud music in the background. The calls were followed by another text message, "Its ok. music too loud."

———

Over the next several minutes, Channy contacted Brittany's other friends, Jessica Perry and Elizabeth Hernandez. After trying Brittany's phone with no answer, Elizabeth called Perez's girlfriend, Dorothy. Dorothy Maraglino told Elizabeth she knew nothing about a dinner cruise and hadn't spoken to Brittany at all that day. An obvious lie.

At 8:40 P.M., Jessica Perry called Perez, who answered the call. He told Jessica that he and Brittany had driven to downtown San Diego and went to The Whiskey Girl club in the Gaslamp District. He told her that Brittany had met a couple of Marines there and he'd left her there. Jessica Perry knew this couldn't possibly be true - that would have been completely out of character for Brittany. The truth was that she never made it out of Fallbrook.

———

Louis Perez and Dorothy Maraglino took efforts to cover their tracks. Dorothy had worked for a cell phone company in the past and knew that cell phones were traceable. She instructed Perez to drive toward downtown San Diego with Brittany's phone. During the drive, he sent text messages to her phone reading, "Where are you?" and "Your friends are calling me worried." He also messaged Dorothy asking how her night was going, to which she replied, "Just having a quiet night at home."

At 10:10 P.M., Channy tried to call Brittany one more time. When she got no response, she sent a text, "Should I just call the cops?" Channy received a text reply, "I'm ok." Perez then dumped Brittany's phone on the streets of downtown San Diego.

As he drove back to Fallbrook from San Diego, Perez called Brittany's friend Jessica Perry. Trying to establish an alibi, he told her he had been driving around the Gaslamp District looking for Brittany, but finally gave up.

Saturday morning was agonizing for Channy, Elizabeth, and Jessica Perry. There was still no word from their friend. Jessica called Dorothy and told her she knew she had lied to her. She knew that she had spoken to Brittany the previous day. Nervous, Dorothy stammered an excuse and handed the phone to Perez. He hadn't planned his alibi very well and mumbled several conflicting scenarios of what had happened the previous night.

Channy and Elizabeth went to Brittany's apartment, but there was no trace of her and they called the Sheriff's department. When the Sheriff's deputy called Perez he was clearly startled, but offered to come to Brittany's apartment to talk.

When Perez arrived at the apartment, Channy and Elizabeth were still there speaking to the deputy. Perez claimed that when he had picked Brittany up that night, she had already been drinking and was very flirty with him. Channy and Elizabeth immediately rebuffed this and let the deputy know that this was a lie. Perez claimed that he had left Brittany at a club in the Gaslamp District where she flirted with a few Marines. He said that when he couldn't find her, he texted her before he left and she replied with a text saying, "I'm okay."

The deputy's suspicion grew when he asked Perez to show him the text on his phone, but the text wasn't there. There was also the question of his white Ford Explorer parked outside; the bumper and running board of the vehicle were caked with mud. The deputy asked for his consent to a voluntary search of the vehicle and Perez agreed. Inside the vehicle was an AR-15 assault rifle which had been stolen from Camp Pendleton and was illegal in California. Perez was arrested on the weapons charge.

———

That Saturday afternoon, Brittany's mother, Michelle Wrest, got a phone call from her daughter's cell phone. A stranger on the other end of the phone explained that a homeless man had found her phone on the streets of San Diego and was attempting to sell it. Brittany's mother was unaware that her daughter was missing, but assumed the worst and called authorities.

————

On April 15, deputies began their search of the home at 317 East Fallbrook Street where Louis Perez, Dorothy Maraglino, and Jessica Lopez lived. Maraglino and Lopez stood in the front yard and watched. When police arrived the following day to continue the search, Maraglino and Lopez were gone, as was Maraglino's truck. Detectives noticed that several items that were in the house the previous day had been removed.

Law enforcement throughout Southern California were alerted to be on the lookout for Maraglino's Nissan Titan with the license plate, "IVNS KTN." Meanwhile, forensic teams were analyzing Perez's Ford Explorer. Inside his SUV police found blue latex gloves, a large piece of clear plastic sheeting with smeared blood on it, a plastic bag, and a stun baton. Brittany Killgore's DNA was found on the plastic sheeting and latex gloves. Perez's DNA was found on the strap and handle of the stun baton, while more of Brittany's DNA was found on the prongs.

The morning of April 17, Maraglino's truck was spotted in the parking lot of the Ramada Inn near the San Diego airport. According to the front desk, room 105 was registered to Dorothy Maraglino. When police knocked on the door, there was no answer, but officers could hear faint sounds. It sounded like the light cries of a woman.

When the door was forced open, they found a half-naked woman wearing only a red skirt and combat boots. She was bleeding from several deep, self-inflicted wounds on her neck and wrist. The bedsheets were soaked with blood. Several large knives and an orthodontic scalpel were found near the sink next to an empty bottle of Chambord liqueur. At the foot of the bed was a red dog collar with a tag that read, "Rosalin. Property of Ms. Dee." It wasn't Dorothy; it was Jessica Lopez, Dorothy's slave. Lopez was rushed to the hospital and subsequently arrested.

In the room was a clothes hanger above the vanity desk with a note clipped to it that read, "PIGS READ THIS!" Below the note were three envelopes. One was addressed to "Master Ivan," another to "My parents," and the third to a local television station. Each envelope contained a copy of a seven-page suicide note penned by Lopez.

In the suicide note, Lopez claimed it was her that killed Brittany, not Perez or Maraglino, stating, "You've got the WRONG FUCKING PERSON!" The letter claimed that Maraglino and Perez were asleep upstairs while she alone murdered Brittany. She described Brittany as a "miserable cunt" that came between Perez and Maraglino and went into detail of how she killed her.

According to Lopez, she used a Taser to knock her down, then restrained her legs and wrists before gagging her mouth. She then claimed to have tied a rope around her neck where she repeatedly applied and released pressure until she was dead. She then attempted to dismember her body with power tools, washed her body with bleach, and dumped her on the side of a road near Lake Skinner. Officers were immediately dispatched to the Lake Skinner area.

Lopez's letter went on about her love for Dorothy Maraglino, her mistress. Using the hotel's surveillance cameras, police were able to see that Maraglino had been in the room when Lopez wrote the notes. Lopez took the first copy of the note to the hotel receptionist to make the copies. Maraglino left the hotel that morning and boarded a plane to Virginia.

Certain statements in the note, however, made no sense. Lopez wrote that the murder happened after 11:15 P.M. From the string of text messages, police already knew that was unlikely. Lopez also claimed that Brittany, who didn't drive, "suddenly appeared" at the house at 317 East Fallbrook Street unannounced and demanded sex from Perez.

———

Later that day, a maintenance worker clearing brush about a mile south of Lake Skinner found the nude body of Brittany Killgore dumped in a ditch.

The bruising on Brittany's wrists revealed that she had been bound with handcuffs. Five small marks on the left side of her face were an exact match for the pins of the stun baton. Deep postmortem wounds on her knee showed that someone had unsuccessfully attempted to dismember her body parts with a power saw.

The cartilage surrounding her trachea had been crushed. By examining the hemorrhaging in her eyes, the medical examiner could tell that pressure had been applied and released repeatedly over a long period, just as Jessica Lopez wrote in her suicide note. Ultimately, the cause of death was ligature strangulation.

As lead detective Brian Patterson drove to the spot where the body was dumped, he received a call from Dorothy Maraglino who was still on the run. Attempting to establish an alibi, she told him that she and Lopez were home that night and rented "The Adventures of Rin Tin Tin." Patterson, however, was more interested in the flaws in both Perez's and Lopez's stories. When he questioned her on the inconsistencies, she hung up.

Two days after they found the body, police searched Maraglino's house once again. This time they found the roll of plastic that Lopez mentioned in her note and a blade from a reciprocating saw.

Detectives also found several BDSM photos, videos, documents, sex toys, and bondage equipment. One document recovered was a "release of liability" form. It was a contract stating that Dorothy Maraglino agreed to voluntarily endure Louis Perez's beatings, whippings, and asphyxia, and that he held no responsibility in the case of "injuries or loss of life."

They also found a document in which Maraglino released her anger to Perez, encouraging him to "deliver justice on her behalf." The letter, riddled with strange spellings, was written by Maraglino on the day Brittany had been murdered,

> "I Dee do hereby give to Ivan all my grudges and revenge
> from my birth till now. I release my anger and entrust justice
> into Ivan's hands. I accept Ivan will decide, design, and
> dispense the measure of restribution he deems appropriate
> to my enemies, tormentors, and violators." (Signed, "Dee")

Another document read, "Please consider accepting this gift. I leave all methods of retribution to you. Please distroy them all. Rape the women. Destroy their reputation. Take their posessions. When you deem, take their last breath. I release all I carry from my rapist, abuseas, and tormentors to you. I'll join in where you direct me and allow, but I realse my own will and agenda in these matters." (Signed "Kitten")

Yet another document written by Maraglino detailed a fantasy she had of coming up behind a person and slitting their throat.

Other items found in the house included nylon rope with hairs embedded in it, duct tape, plastic bags, a rope and pulley system, a Black & Decker saber saw, and a red Skill saw.

Dorothy Maraglino was arrested on May 10, 2012, and returned to San Diego. Perez was still in custody on the weapons charge. All three suspects were charged with first-degree murder, conspiracy to commit kidnapping, kidnapping, torture, and attempted sexual battery by restraint.

With the three defendants in custody, the prosecution began their analysis of the evidence to prepare for trial. Detectives found profiles for both Perez and Maraglino on BDSM websites BMEhookups.com and TSRnetwork.com where "Ivan" described himself as "Lord and Master," and Dee as "slave, lover, confidant and partner." On another website, he wrote,

> "I am lord and master, dom and daddy of my house. My
> slave, Ms. Dee, is a slave to no one, but myself."

Dee's profile described herself as "an Alpha slave to Master Ivan."

Their profiles showed that they were looking for additional sex slaves and other couples to join their family: "We have a poly home in which I own two slave girls. Life is good." ("Poly" is referring to a polyamorous relationship involving multiple sexual partners, in this case one which is open to new individuals.)

Dorothy Maraglino was pregnant with Perez's baby when police arrested her. Perez requested that when the baby was born, she give custody to a friend of his named Becky Zagha. Zagha visited both Perez and Maraglino in prison regularly before the baby was born and Maraglino agreed to give custody of the baby to Zagha.

According to Maraglino, the agreement was that she would continue to live in the San Diego area and bring the child in for weekly jail visits. When the baby was born, however, Zagha took custody of the baby and moved to central California. The prison visits stopped. Maraglino tried in vain to regain custody of the child and give custody to her family on the east coast, but the courts sided with Zagha.

On one of Zagha's visits to Perez, he admitted to her that "everybody had a role to play that night, including myself." Although Perez later claimed he was referring to the cover-up, not the murder, that statement would later be used against all three of them in court.

The prosecution had a dilemma: Jessica Lopez's confession letter was an important piece of evidence, but her intention was to exonerate Perez and Maraglino. Introducing the letter into evidence was risky. They needed to establish that the letter was evidence of Lopez's guilt, but also prove that it wasn't evidence that Perez and Maraglino were innocent.

Another document that detectives seized was initially thought to be useless as it was written in some sort of code. Using a Forensic Document Examiner and the FBI Crypt-analysis Unit to decipher the code, it revealed a detailed plan to kidnap, torture, and murder a friend of Jessica Lopez.

Over 3,000 jury summons were mailed throughout San Diego county. During jury selection, potential jurors were warned of the unspeakable horrors they would hear of during testimony. During the jury selection process, many potential jurors broke down in tears and asked to be relieved of duty.

The murder trial started on September 8, 2015, and all three defendants were tried together. The prosecution was careful not to take Lopez's admission of the murder as absolute truth and never indicated who exactly was responsible for Brittany's death. Instead, they placed equal blame on each defendant.

Ultimately, it was cell phone records that were the key piece of evidence against the three of them. Cell phone data showed that Brittany did not show up at Maraglino's home unannounced, as Lopez claimed. The text messages that were sent to Brittany's friends that evening were all sent from inside Maraglino's house. Video evidence from the apartment complex also proved that Perez picked her up that evening and she never made it out of Fallbrook: she was taken straight to their home at 317 East Fallbrook Street.

During the trial, Perez took the stand in his own defense. He admitted that he tricked Brittany into believing they were going on a dinner cruise. He also admitted that he took her cell phone to downtown San Diego and dumped it. He denied, however, the accusation that he dumped the phone to give Maraglino and Lopez more time to clean up the crime scene.

Each defendant eventually turned on the other. Jessica Lopez claimed she was just playing the role of the obedient slave and her only crime was writing the suicide/confession letter to protect her master and mistress. Dorothy Maraglino claimed that because she was pregnant, she had put all of her BDSM activities on hold. She claimed that she only helped cover up the crime and that Lopez was the sole killer. Perez also blamed Lopez, citing the confession letter. He argued that he only helped with the cover-up.

The trial lasted six weeks and the jury deliberated for three days. Eventually the jury found Dorothy Maraglino, Louis Perez, and Jessica Lopez each guilty of first-degree murder, torture, and kidnapping. Perez and Maraglino were also found guilty of conspiracy to commit kidnapping.

The death penalty was initially considered, but later ruled out. All three received two life sentences in California state prison without the possibility of parole.

Dorothy Maraglino writes on prisonwriters.com of her complaints of the California prison system, bemoaning her bunkmate's body odor, the bad food, and her suicide attempts. Maybe she should have thought about what prison might be like before she snuffed out the life of an innocent girl. If you'd like to read her rants, a link is provided in the online appendix at the end of this book.

———

Years later, the house at 317 East Fallbrook Street fell into foreclosure. It later sold to a couple in their thirties for $212,000 who had no idea that there had been a savage murder in the house. Unfortunately, there was nothing they could do once they found out and kept the house despite its brutal history.

CHAPTER 4
DIVINE JUSTICE

The 1970s were a scary time in the Pacific Northwest - especially if you were a young, cute, teenage girl. It seemed that every month there was news of another young girl that had gone missing.

———

In January 1970, seventeen-year-old Patricia Garrison was murdered as she drove home from her part-time job at SeaFirst Bank in Olympia, Washington. The killer had cut her scalp twenty times with a knife and stabbed her three times in the chest, once in the back of her shoulder, and eight more times on her arms and legs. He then dumped her in front of St. Peter's Hospital, where she clung to life for thirty-two hours before succumbing to her wounds.

Eight months later, three children were playing in a remote wooded area just north of Olympia when they discovered a human skull. The kids kept it as a secret for a day at their clubhouse before telling the police. Near where they found the skull, Thurston county deputies uncovered a shallow grave that had been scavenged by animals. In addition to more bones, they found a piece of scalp with long dark blonde hair, a pair of blue jeans, white sneakers, and a polka-dot swimsuit.

Neighboring Pierce county officials suspected right away that it was the body of a missing thirteen-year-old, Laura Lea Burbank. Laura had been on her way to a pet shop when she had disappeared two months earlier. Detectives already had a suspect — an employee of the pet shop, David Fisher, who had promised to show her some baby raccoons.

Fisher was known to have a predilection for young girls and his wife had found a pair of young girl's underwear in their home. Police quickly arrested Fisher and he was later convicted and sentenced.

Just a few months later, another young Olympia girl, fifteen-year-old Valerie Goode, was shot to death by a stranger in her own home. Over the next several years, many more girls disappeared and were later found butchered.

Some, like nineteen-year-old Debbie Potter who was killed while leaving her job as a waitress at the China Clipper restaurant, were never solved. Several more in the Olympia area - like Lynda Healy, Donna Manson, Susan Rancourt, and Roberta Parks - were later confirmed to be victims of the notorious Ted Bundy.

———

Though she was only fourteen years-old, Kathy Devine was struggling with the reality of becoming a young adult. She had fought with her young boyfriend and naively assumed that the end of the relationship was also the end of the world.

She had cousins that lived in Portland, Oregon, and decided to run away from home. Her plan was to hitchhike from her home on Aurora Avenue North, Seattle, and make her way down to Oregon to stay with her cousins for a while. On November 25, 1973, Kathy packed a small bag and left her mother a note, ending it with, "P.S. Don't worry mom, I'll be back."

Kathy's mother reported her daughter missing to Seattle police immediately after she left, but runaways were common in the seventies. The police informed her that young girls usually come home on their own after a few days and it would be best if she just wait it out.

———

Less than two weeks later, a young couple were cleaning the campground at Camp Margaret McKenney park just south of Olympia. At the edge of a clearing they found the partially clad body of a young girl. Her clothes had been cut with a knife. When police arrived, they found the young girl face-down in the rain. She had been strangled, sodomized, and her throat had been slit. The wound at her throat had been disturbed by animals and the stage of decomposition told medical examiners that she had been there for at least a week. The lack of blood at the scene indicated that the location was a body dump; she had been killed elsewhere.

There was no wallet or purse found at the scene and nothing to identify who the girl was other than the clothes she was wearing. On her body, detectives found a suede coat with a fake fur trim, a white blouse that had been cut open, and dark blue denim jeans that had been cut up the backside. The jeans had a dragon patch on the left rear pocket. She was wearing one brown "waffle stomper" boot, but the other boot was missing. On her ears were a pair of gold cross earrings, and on her fingers she wore a Florentine friendship ring and a blue-green zircon ring.

The location of the campground was very remote. It was more than five miles from Interstate 5 and about fifteen miles south of downtown Olympia, off a rarely traveled side-road flanked with a dense fir and pine forest. Thurston county police assumed the killer must have known the area as it wasn't the type of place a person would just randomly happen upon.

When police showed the items of clothing on the nightly news the following evening, Kathy's older sister Sherrie recognized the dragon patch right away. She knew the family's worst nightmare had come true. Dental records confirmed that the dead girl was Kathy Devine.

Thurston county detectives worked together with Seattle police to attempt to retrace Kathy's steps as she left Seattle. One of Kathy's friends told police they saw her getting into a truck in Seattle near her home, while another friend claimed to have seen her with her boyfriend a few days after she went missing. The first step for investigators was to talk to the ex-boyfriend.

Since he was underage, Seattle police spoke to the parents of Kathy's ex-boyfriend and his parents allowed them to interview the boy. He confirmed that he and Kathy had broken up on November 25, but that this was the last time he had talked to her. Police searched his home and he agreed to take a polygraph. He passed the polygraph and a search of the home provided no clues. The young boy was cleared.

When the news of Kathy's death was released to the public, tips came in from all over the state. One tip in particular seemed odd: a neighbor of the Devine family claimed that he had witnessed Kathy's murder, but when police asked him for more details, he remained silent. With a search warrant in hand, detectives searched the man's home. In the man's house they found several newspaper clippings about the murder. They also found a knife covered in blood which was approximately the same size as the knife that would have been used to slice Kathy's throat. The blood, however, proved to be animal blood, and the man was cleared as a suspect. He was just a bizarre man fixated on the case.

Another tip unfortunately went unnoticed. Police received a call from someone that worked at Restover Truck Stop south of Olympia. The man said that he had suspected a co-worker was stealing from him and looked in the back of his pickup truck. The man claimed that he looked under a tarp in the back of his truck and saw a sleeping bag covered with blood, as well as a small single waffle stomper boot. The following day, the truck was completely and mysteriously burned in a fire. Sadly, the tip was not followed up on at the time.

Detectives were left with only a few clues: the clothes she was wearing and DNA that remained from a vaginal swab. Unfortunately, in 1970 the use of DNA as a crime-solving tool was more than a decade away.

———

Days turned to months and months stretched into years, but there were no new clues. Although the case was going cold, the Thurston county detectives kept the file open. Other young girls were still dying in the area.

In the years that followed, the world became aware of one of the most notorious serial killers in history — Ted Bundy. By

1975 the sociopath had kidnapped, raped, and brutally murdered numerous young women in the same area that Kathy was killed. Bundy's prey were almost always a certain type of girl; young, with long, straight hair parted in the middle. Kathy fit that description to a T.

After his arrest and conviction, Ted Bundy eventually confessed to thirty murders, many of which happened in the same area around Olympia. It was widely believed that Kathy was another one of his victims.

With days left before he was to be electrocuted, Thurston county detectives visited Ted Bundy in prison. With nothing left to lose, they hoped that he might confess to the murder of Kathy Devine and put an end to the mystery. However, they were surprised by his answer. He flatly denied it.

Though many still believed that Bundy did it, detectives knew better. Although Kathy was a similar age and the murder happened in the same area of the country as Bundy's killings, it didn't fit his style. Bundy often beheaded his victims, but Kathy was not beheaded. Also, Kathy was last seen getting into a truck, whereas Bundy usually drove a Volkswagen Bug and used a sling or a crutch to make himself seem helpless.

Kathy's family, however, spent the next twenty-nine years after her death believing that Ted Bundy had killed their daughter and had gone to his grave with the secret.

———

By 2002, there had been massive advances in crime fighting with the use of DNA. In 1998, the FBI had developed the Combined DNA Index System (CODIS) and made it available at a national level.

The Washington State Patrol Crime Lab was tasked with going through cold cases from the 1970s when Kathy Devine's case eventually came up. Detectives had saved the DNA from the crime scene for twenty-nine years and forensic scientists ran it through CODIS. There was a hit: William Earl Cosden Jr.

————

In 1966, nineteen-year-old William Cosden Jr. had just returned from an eleven-month tour in Vietnam to live with his parents in St. Mary's county, Maryland. Cosden had been injured during combat and given a medical discharge as a "highly decorated" Marine, but in hindsight he may have just had a propensity for killing.

Kathy Devine, William Cosden (1966), & William Cosden (2002)

Just months after his arrival back in the states, Cosden attended a dance in the tiny town of Leonardtown, Maryland. Cosden had his eye on a certain girl: twenty-two-year-old Helen Patricia Pilkerton. At the end of the evening, Helen made the biggest mistake of her life. She accepted a ride home from Cosden.

The following morning, two teenage girls found the lifeless body of Helen Pilkerton in a nearby creek. She had been badly beaten, stabbed, and raped with a pool cue. Cosden was quickly arrested for the crime.

The murder trial revealed what Cosden had experienced in Vietnam. The defense argued that his traumatic experiences caused him to develop "homicidal tendencies" and, because of these tendencies, "his conduct was directly and proximately traceable to his combat experience in the United States Marine Corps." Their plan was to plead insanity.

According to court documents, Cosden,

> "participated in the killing of over 200 of the enemy in a single operation... In which he distinguished himself as a fighter." Military doctors noted that he, "suffered from an uncontrollable urge to shoot his fellow Marines."

Despite attempting to choke another patient, Cosden had been released from the Military hospital in Philadelphia only to return to Maryland and murder Helen Pilkerton.

The defense proved that Cosden was not guilty by reason of insanity and he was acquitted of his murder charge. He was sent to the Clifton T. Perkins State Hospital for the Criminally Insane, but within three years authorities believed he had miraculously recovered and Cosden was set free.

After his release in early 1973, Cosden and his parents moved to Washington state where his father purchased the Restover Truck Stop just south of Olympia on Interstate 5.

Cosden worked for his father at the truck stop, the perfect location to prey on young girls.

————

Not long after his arrival in Washington state, Cosden murdered Kathy Devine. It's believed that she had hitchhiked from Seattle down Interstate 5 to the Littlerock/Maytown exit where she encountered Cosden working at his father's truck stop.

After Kathy's body was found, Cosden went completely undetected for two more years until Nov 30, 1975, when twenty-four-year-old Beverly Pearson was on her way home from work in Olympia and stopped to get gas. She often stopped at the Restover Truck Stop and was familiar with Cosden. It was a particularly cold and snowy night and, once cars left the main Interstate, the roads were extremely icy. Cosden offered to follow Beverly home that night in his truck to make sure she made it home safely, but she politely refused. She didn't live far and knew the icy roads well.

As she left the truck stop and continued her drive home, Beverly noticed Cosden's headlights behind her. He had followed her anyway. Suddenly, his headlights swerved off the road and his truck slid off into the ditch. Beverly stopped her truck and slowly reversed to see if he needed help. Cosden asked her to get behind the wheel of his truck and try to drive it out of the ditch while he pushed. That's when he made his move; Cosden struck her over the head with a large rubber mallet, pushed her into his truck, and drove off.

Still conscious, Beverly pleaded for her life, "Please don't hit me again!" She told him that she knew him and she knew his family, trying to communicate with him on a personal level.

Cosden pulled onto on an old logging road, stopped the truck, and raped her twice. Through it all, Beverly calmly kept talking to him, trying to make him understand that she was a human. She asked him personal questions and mentioned that they were neighbors. She begged for her life.

Her plan worked and Cosden eventually drove her back to her truck, sparing her life. Beverly was the stepdaughter of a police detective. As soon as she got home, she called police and reported the sexual assault. For the rape, twenty-nine-year-old Cosden was tried, convicted, and sentenced to forty-eight years in prison and was to receive extensive psychiatric treatment.

———

Cosden sat in prison for twenty-six years before the Washington State Patrol Crime Lab linked his DNA to Kathy Devine's murder. When confronted with the evidence against him, Cosden admitted he had sex with Kathy but claimed it was consensual and that he didn't kill her.

During the murder trial, jurors weren't allowed to hear about his past rape conviction or his prior murder trial and insanity plea. Despite this disadvantage for the prosecution, Cosden was found guilty of first-degree murder and sentenced to life in prison.

On June 23, 2015, William Earl Cosden Jr. died of a sudden heart attack while in prison.

CHAPTER 5
THE AMISH KILLER

I n the early 1990s, Rockdale Township was a tiny area in the northwest corner of Pennsylvania with only about 1,000 residents, many of which were Old Order Amish. However, in the years since the tragedy of March 18, 1993, much of the Amish community of Rockdale has moved away from the area in an attempt to escape the horrific legacy of Ed Gingerich.

———

Ed Gingerich was born in 1963 in Norwich, Ontario, Canada, into an Old Order Amish family. The Amish way of life was ever-changing. While they were slow to adopt modern technology, they would eventually adapt under certain circumstances.

The Amish people believed in a simplistic, uncomplicated way of life: plain clothing and traditionalist Swiss/German Anabaptist Christian beliefs. Many of the modern conveniences that most of us see as a part of everyday life were not allowed by the Amish. Hard work, family time, and face-to-face conversations were cherished. Any person that was not Amish was referred to as "English," regardless of their actual ethnicity.

As a teenage boy, Ed Gingerich worked in his father's wood shop with the simple machines that the Amish allowed themselves. Through the years, he became increasingly curious about more complicated machinery and devices that were not allowed in the Amish faith. Frustrated with the simple life, Ed eventually grew defiant and rebellious. He complained about having to constantly do mundane chores and lost any interest in going to church.

Early on it was obvious to others that Ed wasn't the same as the other Amish people in the community. Most Amish children would marry by their late teens, but when Ed had not found a match by his early twenties, Bishop Rudy Shetler - who was the leader of the community - had a solution. His niece, Katie Shetler, also had yet to marry and her faith in the Amish life was unwavering. The Bishop and members of the community believed Katie would be a good influence for the troubled young man.

Ed Gingerich

Katie saw potential in Ed. She felt sure that she could change his ways and fell deeply in love with him. Though Ed was reluctant, the Bishop pushed the couple into marriage. Many of the elders of the community didn't trust Ed, but they hesitantly approved the marriage in hopes that Katie could bring him back to a more traditional way of life.

Katie and Ed were married on December 2, 1986, in an uneventful Amish ceremony with ordinary plain clothes and no wedding rings. Ten months later, the couple had their first child, Dannie, but neither fatherhood nor married life seemed to interest Ed.

Ed's work provided him brief contact with English people from outside the Amish community. Through a man named Dave Lindsey, he learned about the fascinating world outside of his tiny perspective. Dave was a devout evangelical Christian and told Ed stories of Satan and Hell. Dave explained to Ed that if he continued to follow the Amish faith, he and his family would burn in Hell for all eternity.

Shortly after the birth of their son, Ed grew more and more lethargic and fell into a deep depression. He spoke less and less often and, when he did, it was usually to whine or berate his wife. Katie often had a hard time getting him out of bed to go to work.

Frustrated, Katie went to her uncle, Bishop Shetler, for help. Although Ed was clearly showing signs of depression, the Amish people had very little experience with mental health issues. Further complicating matters, the Amish didn't believe in the healing powers of modern medicine – instead, they were convinced that God alone had the power to heal.

Bishop Shetler presumed Ed's problems were physical and took him to Merritt Terrell, a chiropractor in nearby Cambridge Springs. Believing it would purify his blood, Mr. Terrell's "prescription" was to give him scalp massages and have him eat blackstrap molasses.

Three more years passed by. Ed and Katie had another son, Enos, and a daughter, Mary, but his depression only escalated. Eventually his anger became physical and family members noticed Katie doing her best to hide her bruises.

At work, Ed spent more time with people from outside the Amish faith and he drifted further and further away from the community. Eventually, he confided to Katie that he had doubts about the Amish faith and was worried that the whole family would be banished to Hell.

By the spring of 1992, Katie and Ed's brothers Atlee and Joe sought psychiatric help for Ed when he began to hallucinate. He told his wife he saw giant rabbits. He would howl like a wolf and spit on the ceiling, claiming there were eyes all over him, watching him. He began ranting that God and Satan were fighting for his soul; he jumped out of their second story house window and ran down the dirt road.

Though it was against the Amish way, twice the family called 911 and had him hospitalized. On one occasion, it took seven men to hold him down and hog-tie him in order to get him to the hospital, but when they untied him he flailed about, smashing medical equipment.

Eventually, Ed was diagnosed with paranoid schizophrenia and given anti-psychotic drugs to calm him. Many of the Amish townspeople just believed that Ed was paying the price for his sinful ways. God was punishing him.

Ed took the drugs but complained about the side-effects. He said they made him walk around in a stupor and he was unable to think straight. The Bishop and the elders of the community made a decision to let him stop taking the drugs, but the hallucinations and voices in his head continued.

———

On March 18, 1993, Ed threatened suicide, ranting that Satan was trying to steal his soul and that he thought Katie was the devil. There was a wedding planned that evening and he was upset that Katie believed he wasn't well enough to attend. Ed asked an English neighbor to take him to the chiropractor once again.

Early that evening after the chiropractor visit, Ed woke from a nap, walked into the kitchen, and punched Katie in the face in front of their six-year-old son Dannie. Katie fell to the floor and yelled for Dannie to run and get help. Dannie ran over a mile to Ed's brother's house while Ed calmly walked out to the back porch and put on his work boots. Their other children, Mary and Enos, stayed in the room to witness the horror that was to come.

Ed's younger brother Daniel raced to the house on horse-back. When he opened the door, he saw Ed sitting on Katie's body with a look of insanity on his face. Katie's head was a mush of skull and brains on the floor. He had stomped her head into a pulp of nothingness.

Daniel claimed that he saw the devil standing next to his brother and was scared for his own life. Terrified, he ran down the road to a non-Amish neighbor's house to call 911.

Meadville police arrived at dusk to find Ed Gingerich covered in blood, walking calmly down Sturgis Road. He was carrying his daughter Mary in one arm and his son Enos was walking by his side, holding his hand. Ed was immediately taken into custody.

When police entered the house, they realized that Ed had disemboweled her while his brother ran for help. Her torso was cut from her throat to just below her navel and all of her organs had been piled to the side of her body. He had gutted her like a hunter would gut a deer. Police and EMT workers later said the mess on the floor wasn't even recognizable as human.

————

Late that night, detectives began interviewing Ed.

Ed: "I'm just like in a tunnel."

Detective: "I want to try and understand this. Exactly what happened. Why you killed Katie."

Ed: "Because, for some reason, I felt... what is going to happen after we die? For some reason, I think we could still save her."

Detective: "No, we cannot. I've seen Katie and we cannot save her. Katie is dead and you know Katie is dead."

Ed: "Yeah, I know. Why did I kill her? I felt it was a gain."

Detective: "A gain for who?"

Ed: "A gain for us people."

Detective: "All the people?"

Ed: "Yeah, not just my religion."

Detective: "Maybe you can explain to me why you felt that you had to remove Katie's brain and work your way from the brain down. Explain that to me."

Ed: "You know how we, the human beings were made?"

Detective: "Yeah. From the top down?"

Ed: "That's right. I had it in my mind that if I worked from the top down... I'm so lost, I don't know what to say."

Detective: "We're getting away from why you felt that you had to kill Katie."

Ed: "To get rid of the devil."

Detectives interviewed Ed for more than an hour, most of which was nonsensical ramblings about how he thought Katie was the devil. Half of the time he was aware that he had killed her, but at other times he seemed to have no recollection of the night at all.

Ed Gingerich was the first Amish person to ever be charged with murder, but at trial was found, "guilty of involuntary manslaughter but mentally ill."

Had he been found guilty by reason of insanity, Gingerich could have been allowed indefinite hospitalization, but the conviction only carried a maximum of five years. Ed served his sentence in the State Correctional Institution in Mercer, Pennsylvania, and he was given credit for the time he had already served awaiting trial.

After serving the full five-year sentence, thirty-four-year-old Gingerich was free. Because he was not found to be insane, his ongoing treatment was his own responsibility. Almost sixty members of the Brownhill Amish community signed a petition requesting his permanent commitment to a mental hospital, but their pleas fell on deaf ears.

> "We like Ed Gingerich but absolutely don't trust him and are seriously afraid of him."

While the Brownhill Amish community wanted to see him in a mental institution, other Amish communities were happy to see him released and welcomed him, thinking they could help him. They believed he was sorry for the things he had done and required forgiveness to repent his sins. After his release, Ed was accepted into an Amish mental health facility in Michigan. However, after an episode where he had stopped taking his medication, he was again moved to a psychiatric unit in Indiana where he could receive constant supervision.

Throughout the years, Ed desperately wanted to reconcile with his children and family. It was all he thought about. In

2007, he returned to Crawford county and rented a house near the Brownhill Amish community.

Still diligently taking his meds and seeing a psychiatrist and caseworker regularly, Ed reconciled with his two brothers and his two sons. Mary, however, lived with her grandparents and was forbidden from seeing her father.

Word eventually got around to the Brownhill community of Ed's reconciliation, which resulted in the "shunning" of his sons who had become teenagers. Shunning is a decision made by the church to exclude a person and cease interaction for not following the rules set by the church.

Though reconciled with his sons, Ed was desperate to reconcile with his daughter Mary, who was now seventeen and looked very much like her mother. In April 2007, while she was riding in a buggy, Ed and his brothers abducted Mary and took her to a relative's home in the neighboring McKean county. The Brownhill community worried that Ed plotted to kill his daughter, but after spending five days with her father, she was returned safely.

Ed was arrested for the abduction and pleaded no contest. He was sentenced to six months of probation and fined $500. The following year, Ed was arrested again when he was caught deer hunting with a rifle. His felony conviction prevented him from owning or using a firearm. Ed again pleaded guilty and served three more months in jail.

Although they loved their brother, Ed's brothers Joe and Atlee reconciled with the Brownhill community. The community would only accept them back if they stopped seeing Ed. Ed moved in with another cousin in another town, but when their English neighbors protested against a killer moving into their area, he was again asked to leave.

With nowhere left to turn, Ed moved in with the attorney that represented him at trial, George Schroeck. George and his wife Stephanie lived on a farm in nearby Cambridge Springs. Although Ed worked on the farm and continued taking his anti-psychotic and anti-depressant drugs, he was still extremely depressed. The Schroecks said Ed never had an episode while living with them, but was lethargic about having no contact with his family.

On the morning of January 14, 2011, Ed Gingerich went out to the barn to feed the horses, but when he hadn't returned five hours later, Stephanie went out to check on him. Ed had hung himself from a rafter in the barn. In the dust on top of the bucket that he had kicked out from underneath himself, he wrote, "Forgive me please."

Although the Amish community had shunned Ed Gingerich in life, they forgave him in death. Bishop Rudy Shelter, Katie's uncle, preached at the funeral held at his brother Atlee's home. Amish people came from several states to attend. He lies buried next to his wife in the Grabhof Amish Cemetery.

CHAPTER 6
COLD STORAGE KILLER

Among the popular beach towns along the Pacific coast, between Los Angeles and San Diego, lies Newport Beach. Located in the middle of Orange County, Newport Beach was known for its seven tiny manmade islands housing expensive mansions, many with their own docks and yachts as expensive as the homes. The area is protected by Balboa peninsula, a long stretch of land that encapsulates the islands and creates a natural harbor.

Although she didn't live in one of the mansions, twenty-three-year-old Denise Huber did live with her parents in an upscale neighborhood of Newport Beach. Her shoulder-length straight brown hair and striking blue eyes made her very popular with the boys. Denise first met Steve Horrocks when she worked at the Old Spaghetti Factory on the Balboa peninsula in 1987. Steve was a bartender and she was a waitress.

Though they weren't romantically involved at the time, four years later in 1991, Denise and Steve started dating. Steve still worked at the Old Spaghetti Factory and Denise had graduated from the University of California at Irvine with a degree in social sciences. The job market was tight at the time and she couldn't find a job in her field. She took another waitressing job at the Cannery Seafood restaurant and worked part-time as a cashier at The Broadway department store.

On the afternoon of June 2, 1991, Steve won two free tickets to see the singer Morrissey later that evening. The concert was being held at The Forum, a venue in Inglewood, nearly an hour north in Los Angeles county. Unfortunately Steve had to work that night, so he suggested Denise and his friend Rob Calvert go together. Denise was also good friends with Rob, so the two agreed to go to the concert together.

After the concert, Denise and Rob decided to stop for a drink at the El Paso Cantina in Long Beach. Once there, they called Steve and invited him to meet them, but he declined. He had just gotten off work and was trying to save money.

While having late-night drinks, Denise and Rob ran into an acquaintance of Denise's named Ross. Denise knew that Ross had had a crush on her for years. Ross asked Denise if he could speak to her privately outside. When Denise returned, she explained to Rob that Ross had asked her out and she'd turned him down.

Rob and Denise stayed at El Paso Cantina until they closed after 1:00 A.M., then drove toward home. Denise dropped Rob off at his home in Huntington Beach just after 2:00 A.M. and continued her drive.

The drive from Huntington Beach to Denise's home in the East Bluff neighborhood of Newport Beach ran along Highway 1, the Pacific Coast Highway. However, when her parents awoke the next morning, they realized that Denise never made it home that night.

Denise Huber

It wasn't unheard of for Denise to stay out all night. After all, she was twenty-three years old - but it was extremely out of character for her to not let her parents know.

Panicked, her parents - Dennis and Ione Huber - called Denise's friend Tammy Brown. Although Tammy had known that she had gone to the concert, she hadn't heard from her since. Tammy gathered several friends and, alongside Denise's parents, they both set out to look for her.

They had searched the whole day, but there was no sign of Denise. Just before sundown that evening, Tammy located Denise's car parked in the southbound lane along Highway 73, the Corona del Mar highway. It was just a few miles from her parents' home.

The gray 1988 Honda Accord had been abandoned. The right rear tire was flat, the windows were rolled down, and the doors were unlocked. The battery had been drained and it was evident that the headlights and emergency flashers had been on all night.

When police arrived on the scene, they found no sign of a struggle, no blood, and nothing to indicate there had been foul play. The stretch of highway was in a busy area with plenty of businesses nearby and several call boxes where she could have called for help, but didn't. Still, there was no sign of Denise.

Her keys, purse, and wallet were not found at the scene and there were no signs of tampering with the tire. The sidewall had failed and there were skid marks showing that it had indeed blown out. Everything indicated that she had pulled over and walked off of the freeway to find help. But one thing was troubling... there were no fingerprints in the car — not even her own. It was obvious that it had been wiped clean.

Despite the car being wiped down, police initially believed she had possibly run off with a boyfriend without notifying her parents. Dennis and Ione, however, knew this wasn't the case and were hit with an unescapable sense of dread. Their daughter had been taken against her will.

Although Robert Calvert, Steve Horrocks, and Ross - the young man that asked her out at the bar that night - were all initially suspects, they were all cooperative and had alibis. They were quickly eliminated.

Police were left with very few clues. They did what they could: they used helicopters to search the immediate area and trained dogs to find her scent, but were ultimately left with nothing to go on. She had simply vanished.

Denise's parents turned to the public for help. They raised $10,000 in donations to offer a reward for the return of their daughter. They placed a huge thirty-foot banner on the side of an apartment building that faced the freeway where her car was found. They were looking for any information at all from anyone that may have seen their daughter on the side of the road that night.

Giant aerial banners were pulled behind planes and they placed billboards all over the area. Tips came in, but nothing seemed to help.

Denise's parents never gave up hope. Her father's car became a rolling billboard. When he was in public and he saw a tall girl with long brown hair on the street, he would have to stop to see her face and make sure it wasn't Denise.

The story of the missing girl was run on both local news and nationally, on Inside Edition and America's Most Wanted. At a loss for options, the family accepted the help of unsolicited psychics, but nothing helped. They even took the family dog to the scene where the car was. According to Dennis, the dog "went crazy" and picked up her scent. He followed the dog through a hole in the fence along the highway and to a hotel room at the nearby Marriott Courtyard Hotel. Police followed the lead, but this too was a dead end.

The Huber family hired a private investigator who clashed with detectives. The private investigator believed that Denise had been abducted elsewhere and her car had been placed on the Corona del Mar Freeway as a distraction. After all, Denise was traveling from Huntington Beach to Newport Beach. She wouldn't have needed to go that far inland to get home; she normally would have taken the Pacific Coast highway.

Three years went by with no additional clues. Police checked Denise's dental records against every unidentified body that was found, but by that point the likelihood of Denise ever being found dead or alive was extremely slim.

Eventually, Denise's parents gave up hope and moved to North Dakota. On the third anniversary of her disappearance, Denise's mother told the Los Angeles Times:

> "As time goes by, I realize Denise is probably not alive. Just to know and not have to wonder what happened would be easier than this mystery."

————

Prescott, Arizona, lies halfway between the Phoenix Valley and the mountains of Flagstaff. Its small-town, old-west feel was a welcome respite from the scorching July heat of Phoenix. Elaine and Jack Court were visiting the Prescott Swap Meet and looking to buy some paint for their paint supply business when they met thirty-four-year-old John Famalaro.

Famalaro was working as a self-employed house painter and had been selling paint at the swap meet. Famalaro told Jack and Eliane that he had much more paint to sell them and invited them to his home after the swap meet ended for the day.

When Elaine and Jack arrived at his house, they were a bit surprised. Famalaro was clearly a hoarder. Though he lived in a nice house located in the Prescott Country Club, it was cluttered with junk. From floor to ceiling, the entire house was filled with random items, deteriorating cardboard boxes, and hundreds of paint cans.

Elaine and Jack purchased the paint they needed and, as they left the property, they noticed a twenty-four-foot Ryder rental truck parked in the driveway. Weeds that had grown to waist-height around the truck made it obvious that it had been there for quite some time. Not only was it out of place parked in the driveway, but they noticed that there was a very long electrical extension cord leading from the house into the back of the truck.

Jack knew that truck rental companies didn't usually sell trucks to the public without painting over the logo on the side and asked Elaine to jot down the license plate number before she and Jack left. The couple assumed the truck was stolen and when they got back to Phoenix, notified a friend who was a Phoenix Police detective.

Jack and Elaine's assumptions were correct. When the Yavapai County Sheriff Department searched for the license plate, the truck had indeed been stolen. It was originally rented in California and never returned. The extension cord leading into the rear of the truck most likely meant that it was being used as a methamphetamine lab. Prepared for a drug raid, Sheriff's deputies paid a visit to John Famalaro's home.

When they opened the back of the Ryder truck, it looked similar to what Jack and Elaine had seen inside of the house. The entire truck was filled with paint cans and cardboard boxes. It wasn't the meth lab they were expecting, but detectives were curious to find what was at the end of the long extension cord.

Pushing aside the boxes and paint cans, the cord led to a large, fifteen-cubic-foot chest freezer at the very back of the truck. Police cut the thick masking tape that held the lid shut and opened it. Inside, they found something wrapped in large black plastic bags and a few smaller white plastic bags. All the bags seemed to be covering one large item. Initially officers assumed Famalaro was just storing a deer carcass that he had killed, but when they felt part of the black bag, they realized that what they felt was a frozen human arm.

Famalaro's Ryder Truck

As they peeled away parts of the plastic bags, they revealed the frozen body of a young woman. She was crunched into the fetal position with her hands cuffed behind her back. Her body was wrapped in black plastic bags and her head was wrapped in white plastic bags. Beneath the white plastic bags, duct tape covered her mouth and nose. The bottom of the freezer contained a frozen layer of bodily fluids. John Famalaro was immediately taken into custody and charged with first-degree murder.

Assuming the body had been frozen for some time, detectives knew that thawing it would cause rapid decomposition. In order to keep the body intact as long as possible for analysis, the entire freezer was brought to a forensics lab in Phoenix.

The body in the bags was naked except for rings on her fingers. Using a hairdryer, forensic scientists slowly defrosted her fingers first in order to get fingerprints. Slowly and carefully, they were able to get a set of perfect fingerprints before the decomposition made them unreadable. The prints were a match for Denise Huber. Further analysis showed that her skull had been shattered from blunt force trauma.

Armed with a search warrant, police searched Famalaro's home and the home of his mother, who lived next door. His mother, Anne Famalaro, owned both homes. Famalaro's mother was upset that the police were searching her homes and defiantly set up a lawn chair across the street from the homes. She spent the afternoon glaring at the police.

Inside Famalaro's house, detectives found two boxes marked "Christmas" but filled with contents that were anything but festive. The boxes contained the clothing that Denise Huber was wearing the night she went missing: her high-heels, driver's license, credit cards, lipstick, car keys, checkbook, makeup compact, purse, a set of handcuff keys, and a pair of Famalaro's jeans. Also inside one of the boxes was a Montgomery Ward department store receipt for the chest freezer. It showed that he purchased the freezer in California just days after Denise went missing.

Both her clothes and his were covered with blood. DNA later taken from Denise's bone marrow matched the blood on his jeans. Semen stains found on her clothing matched Famalaro's DNA. Denise's high heels had damage to the back side of the heels, a sign that she had been dragged from behind.

In the basement of the house they found a dungeon that Famalaro had built. Hanging in a closet was a Los Angeles

County Sheriff's uniform, but Famalaro had never been a law enforcement officer. They believed he had been using the uniform to gain the trust of women before abducting them.

Also inside the home they found boxes of the same black and white plastic bags which Denise's body was wrapped in, along with a roll of duct tape. Further searches of the home produced a bloody hammer, a roofer's nail puller, and assorted guns and handcuffs. Forensic anthropologists reconstructed her shattered skull, showing that Denise had been beaten on the head with the nail puller thirty-one times. From pieces of white plastic embedded in the skull, they were able to determine that the plastic bags were over her head while she was being beaten.

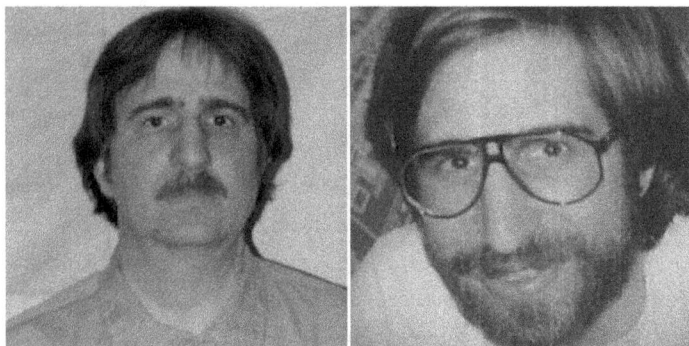

John Famalaro

Detectives were troubled when they found more boxes containing women's clothes that didn't belong to Denise. They believed that this may not have been the first time and Famalaro had possibly done this before. Police brought in cadaver dogs that found a scent which lead straight to the basement. After days of excavating, however, the police found nothing.

One of the boxes marked "Christmas" had an address on it for a rented warehouse space in Laguna Hills, California, just twenty miles from Newport Beach. Detectives found that Famalaro had lived in Newport Beach at the same time Denise went missing and was renting the warehouse space for his painting business.

When detectives entered Famalaro's former warehouse, they noticed a dark stain in the corner on the concrete floor and walls. Detectives sprayed Luminol on the floor and walls of the warehouse, a chemical agent that fluoresces when it comes into contact with the iron compound in blood. The result was positive for massive amounts of blood that matched Denise's DNA.

Prosecutors believed Famalaro posed as a Sheriff's deputy, abducted Denise when her car broke down on the Corona Del Mar freeway, and took her to his nearby Laguna Hills where he raped and bludgeoned her.

———

At trial, there was little doubt of Famalaro's guilt. The forensic evidence against him was undeniable. Forensic scientists testified that they found seven specimens of his sperm in Denise's body. He knew he was going down. Facing the death penalty, Famalaro's best chance was to play the sympathy card - maybe he could get life in prison rather than the death penalty.

Famalaro sobbed as the defense explained that he was a victim of mental and emotional stress brought on by his tyrannical mother and the sexual abuse he endured from his brother, a convicted child molester.

Famalaro's brother, Warren Famalaro, was a reluctant witness at the trial and testified that their mother had indeed pushed their ninety-year-old grandmother down a flight of stairs. However, he flatly denied sexually abusing his brother John. Warren told the jury that John was a frail, sickly little boy with a nervous twitch and was bullied as a child.

He went on to explain that their mother Anne bathed them until they were ten years old and paid specific attention to scrubbing their genitals, explaining that

> "her breathing changed… kind of escalated. It just felt like an energy surge of some kind for her."

He continued by saying that John would have extraordinary mood swings, "just powerhouse, beyond type-A, very top-end manic" and would swing to, "just barely able to breathe or keep his eyes open." He also said that when John's pregnant girlfriend left him and gave up their child for adoption, it "crushed and devastated" him. A main factor for why his girlfriend left him was John's mother, who had threatened to kill her.

Ultimately Famalaro was found guilty of first-degree murder, kidnapping, and sodomy. In September 1977, a jury of nine women and three men recommended that Famalaro be sentenced to death.

Executions in California were halted in 2019 and the last person executed was in 2006. As of the time of writing, John Famalaro currently sits on death row in San Quentin State Prison. Though capital punishment has not been abolished in California, it's likely that John Famalaro will die in prison.

CHAPTER 7
COERCIVE CONTROL

Fifteen-year-old Sally Jenny had never had a boyfriend before she met twenty-two-year-old Richard Challen. Barely old enough to call herself an adult, Sally quickly fell in love with the older boy.

Sally grew up in the 1960s in Surrey, England, just southwest of London. Her four older brothers were all in their teens when she was born and her father died when she was six, leaving her to be raised by her mother. Sally's mother didn't believe in higher-education for girls and thought it was good that she had met a man at such a young age.

Richard Challen was outgoing, energetic, and had a healthy sense of humor. As a boy, his passion for fast cars had gained him a reputation as a "petrol head." That obsession with automobiles led him to buy older cars, fix them up, and sell them for a profit. It wasn't long before he had opened his own garage, selling his cars and making a good living.

From the early years, Sally was committed to their relationship and would stop by his apartment after school to cook and clean for him. Richard, however, wasn't as committed and was still very much interested in other girls, often dating other women behind her back.

When Sally became pregnant at seventeen, Richard wasn't ready to settle down and told her, "It could be anybody's." Devastated at his response, Sally asked her older brothers to take her to London for a late-term abortion.

Later, Sally became suspicious that Richard was seeing another woman. When she questioned him about it, Richard displayed his anger by pulling her down a flight of stairs and throwing her out of the front door of his flat. From that point on, Sally thought twice about grappling with him in similar situations.

Despite everything, Sally happily stayed with Richard. He was the only man she had ever loved or even dated. In June 1979, after ten years of dating, Sally and Richard were married - but not before Richard made her sign a prenuptial agreement.

Richard worked long hours at his car dealership and, before long, they had two boys and moved into a large, beautiful home in the upscale area of Claygate, Surrey. From the outside, they seemed to be a normal, happy family.

Sally & Richard Challen

The couple often hosted dinner parties with other wealthy couples in the area. Richard was known for his sports cars, his favorite being his Ferrari Berlinetta. Sally was known for her heavy drinking, chain smoking, and her excessive chatting. She loved to talk and gossip. However, Sally's faults wore on Richard and he began to berate and criticize her in front of their friends.

Richard liked to brag to his friends about how he would skirt the law. In 1991, he outran the police chasing him in cars and a helicopter while racing his motorcycle. Later, in 2006, he crashed his beloved Ferrari on a racetrack in Belgium. In an attempt to collect insurance money for the loss, he shipped the car back to the United Kingdom and made up a story about getting hit by a semi-truck. His plan didn't work, though, and resulted in a conviction of fraud and a one-year suspended sentence.

In addition to the public berating of Sally, friends and family really started to take notice that there were problems when Richard sent out Christmas cards. Rather than a normal family photo on the front of the cards, Richard arranged a photoshoot of himself with two nude women on the hood of his Ferrari. A similar Christmas card came the following year.

As their two boys grew into their teen years, Sally was the center of the family. Richard was either working long hours at the car dealership or off on a vacation with friends to watch Formula 1 racing. The boys recalled Richard constantly ridiculing their mother, calling her "thunder thighs." Or, when someone complimented her looks, his standard reply was, "You haven't seen her naked!"

On a trip to Los Angeles to visit one of Richard's oldest friends, the friend gave Sally a goodnight hug and kiss, just as he had done for years. Richard didn't take kindly to it. That night, he anally raped her and never spoke to the friend again.

Dinner would often be a point of contention. Had she cooked the right thing? Was it cooked properly? When Richard came home from work in the evening, the atmosphere at the family home changed. Everyone was on edge. Richard made rules for the household, whether he was there or not. The television was not to be used if he wasn't in the house. The same went for the telephones.

Richard and Sally's sex life consisted of whatever he wanted at the time; she didn't have a say in the matter. He would often tell her to go upstairs and "get ready" for him, which meant she needed to wash herself first because he claimed that she smelled. Sally became so self-conscious about it that she went to see a doctor to make sure she didn't have a problem.

Eventually, Richard didn't even try to hide his infidelities anymore. He carried several cell phones, frequented massage parlors, and hired escorts. Suspicious of him, Sally followed him to a brothel just minutes from where she was working at the time. When he exited the building, he saw Sally standing across the street and he ran. When his sons confronted him about his infidelities, he denied everything, telling them that their mother was crazy and drank too much.

When Sally took a job working for the Police Federation, Richard made a new rule: all the money that she made was to go to the running of the household. She was to buy the groceries and pay all the bills.

Eventually, Sally began to show signs of stress. She slept and ate less and less. At their dinner parties, she smoked more, drank more, and endlessly chatted. Within their circle of friends, the Challens became the couple to avoid. If they were going to be at one of the many dinner parties, other couples would cancel, wanting to avoid them.

In late 2009, when the brothel that Richard frequented was raided, it was revealed that it had been staffed with trafficked women. Sally couldn't take anymore and, in November 2009 after thirty-one years of marriage, she moved out. Sally still loved her husband despite it all, but she was a broken woman. She used the money that she had inherited to buy a small house near their family home.

Although it was a horrible life with Richard, she found that she couldn't live without him. Life with Richard was all that Sally had ever known. Over the next several months of separation, she started and cancelled divorce proceedings thirteen times. Eventually she gave up and begged him to take her back.

Richard wasn't opposed to getting back together, but if they were to reconcile, he had a set of terms that she would need to comply to. A "post-nuptial agreement." Sally would need to finalize the divorce and take only a £200,000 settlement (approximately $300,000 at the time). It was an insignificant amount compared to what she would normally have been entitled to. She would also need to agree to never speak to strangers when they went out together; he considered it rude and inconsiderate. She would also agree to stop smoking and never interrupt him when he was speaking. The demands were harsh and clearly only a ploy to get her to agree to take a much smaller settlement.

On a Saturday morning in August 2010, Sally met Richard at the family home only a few blocks from the small home that she had purchased earlier that year. Sally hadn't told any of her family, friends, or even her sons about the possibility that she and Richard may be getting back together. Their plan for the day was to clean the home and prepare to put it on the market. They were expecting to make about £1 million from the sale and had spoken of taking a long trip to Australia together to rekindle their relationship.

Despite the talk of reconciliation, Sally hadn't been herself. She laid awake the prior evening in a rage of jealousy. She had managed to get into Richard's email account and noticed that he had been chatting with a woman named Susan Wilce, who he had met through an online dating service. When Sally met Richard at the family home the next morning, it was all she could think of.

Richard said he wanted breakfast before they started cleaning that morning and suggested that Sally run to the store to get some bacon and eggs. As she left for the store, she had a feeling that Richard was trying to get rid of her. She stopped by her home and the store, then returned to the family home to make breakfast for Richard.

As she made breakfast, she had the opportunity to sneak a look at Richard's cell phone where she listened to a voicemail from Susan Wilce asking him to lunch. Her suspicions were correct. Sally made breakfast, placed it in front of Richard, and confronted him about the voicemail. Richard's reply was, "Don't question me, Sally." As he ate, she walked back to her handbag, pulled out a hammer, and struck him in the back of the head.

Sally had snapped. She had placed the hammer in her handbag when she went back to her own home minutes earlier. She beat Richard in the head with the hammer twenty times as he sat at the kitchen table. When he fell to the floor, she stuffed a dishtowel in his mouth to ensure he stopped breathing. She then tore down some old curtains from the home, wrapped his body in them, and wrote a note saying "I love you, Sally" which she laid on his body. Sally then washed the dishes and drove back home.

The next morning, after driving her son David to work, Sally drove to the southern coast of England. Beachy Head is known for its 550-foot white chalk cliffs which plunge down to the rocky coast of the English Channel below. Its massive cliffs make it one of the most popular suicide spots in the world and Sally intended to end her own life. She parked her car, walked to the edge, and called her cousin to tell her what she had done. A suicide prevention team pleaded with her for hours and eventually talked her away from the cliff.

After Sally was arrested and the forensic team had left the family home, their son David was left to scrub his father's blood splatters from the kitchen table and floor.

———

Ten months later at Sally Challen's trial, she looked like a completely different person. She was missing a front tooth, her hair was messy, and her fingertips were stained yellow from chain-smoking. The jury heard her police interview after she was arrested.

> "I just want to say that on Saturday when I went over there I took the hammer over there from my house. I wasn't thinking I'm gonna go there and I'm gonna kill Richard. I was thinking I'm gonna go there and there's a possibility... depending on what panned out."

> "And the hammer's there and I just pick it up and I use it. I don't know why. I feel that if I can't have him, nobody else can. I don't want anyone else to have him if I can't have him."

> "It all became clear that he was playing a game and something flipped inside my head and that's when I picked up the hammer and hit him over the head repeatedly. I don't know why I did it, I don't know why I had the hammer in my bag. I couldn't stop hitting him, I think it took him by surprise."

Sally pleaded guilty to manslaughter on the grounds of diminished responsibility, but not guilty to murder. The prosecution, however, saw it differently. The fact that she carried the hammer to the house just before she killed Richard showed premeditation.

The prosecution painted Sally as a woman obsessed with jealousy and suspicion. They showed that she had been hacking his emails, text messages, and voicemails. She had even counted his Viagra pills.

When questioned by the prosecution, her standard answer was "I suppose so," "I suppose I did," or "I suppose you're right." She didn't bother to put up a fight. The jury heard nothing of the verbal and mental abuse she endured during their thirty-one years of marriage.

After seven days of trial, the jury unanimously found Sally guilty of murder, not manslaughter as she had hoped. Before he issued her sentence, Judge Critchlow told her,

> "You found yourself being eaten up with jealousy at his friendships with other women. You didn't want that and, as you have said, decided that if you could not have him, nobody would. You are somebody who has killed the only man you had known and loved, and you will have to live knowing what you have done. In my judgement the appropriate sentence here is a minimum of twenty-two years imprisonment."

———

Sally Challen never spoke to her sons, friends, or family about the murder during her time in prison, but they all knew the way Richard treated her and his controlling abuse. They knew she had been a broken woman and had become even more so in prison.

Sally had sat in prison for eight years when her niece Dalla mentioned to her that she had found an organization called "Justice For Women." It was a feminist organization that represented women who had killed violent men as a result of domestic abuse.

In 2015, four years after her conviction, "Coercive Control" (controlling or coercive behavior in an intimate or family relationship) had become a crime in the United Kingdom. This meant that Richard's years of controlling behavior offered a glimmer of hope that her murder conviction could be reduced to manslaughter. After much persuasion, Sally wrote a letter to human rights lawyer Harriet Wistrich of Justice For Women.

> "Dear Harriet, I wrote as Dalla told me that you might be prepared to look at my case and let me know if there were any possible grounds of appeal against my conviction for murder. What I did was very wrong. I've always freely admitted that I did kill my husband Richard, but the full circumstances and history were not put before the jury."

Harriet Wistich took Sally's case and prepared for appeal. Together, they listed the abuses by Richard; the instance when he raped her in Los Angeles after his friend kissed her, the Christmas cards with topless girls, the times when he told her to "get ready" and wash up for sex, the post-nuptial agreement, his excursions to a brothel with trafficked women. The list went on and on.

Sally's friends, family, and two sons rallied around her to help with her appeal. Her lawyers argued that Richard's years of control and emotional abuse wore her down and led her to kill. They argued that Sally suffered from an undiagnosed personality disorder at the time of the killing, which was confirmed by psychiatrists while she was in prison.

In a landmark case in the United Kingdom, Sally Challen's conviction was overturned and she was set free in April 2019. Despite all the abuse, Sally still says she loves and misses her husband very much.

CHAPTER 8
THE WEREWOLF BUTCHER

Okanogan county was the largest county in Washington state, lying at the upper-middle of the state along the Canadian border. In the center of the county was the town of Tonasket. With less than 1,000 residents, not much happened in the tiny town, let alone the nearby Aeneas Valley that stretches for miles in each direction around it.

About fifteen miles from Tonasket, Dana Davis lived in a small rural home with her four children. Though the home had no running water, no telephone, and only a generator for power, nine-year-old Penny Davis loved that it sat near the banks of Patterson Creek, where she liked to explore.

In the late afternoon of September 17, 1994, Penny had been playing along the river with her seven-year-old brother. Later that evening when the young boy came back home without his sister, Dana became worried. The boy told his mother that Penny had just walked off and didn't come back.

Dana searched the area up and down Patterson Creek for hours on horseback, but there was no sign of her. By midnight, she had lost hope of finding her daughter without help and drove the fifteen miles into town to report her missing. Penny had simply disappeared without a trace.

By morning a full-scale search was underway. Penny was a tiny girl with blonde hair, hazel eyes, and a small scar on her right knee. She had been wearing a flowery white t-shirt and purple stretch pants with bright yellow stripes. Police, fire-fighters, ambulance members, and sniffer dogs searched the area with local townspeople for days with no clues whatsoever.

Dana remembered that Penny had once skipped school with another girl from Tonasket, but when police checked with the other girl's family, no one had heard from her. Police initially assumed that Penny had just lost her way and they would eventually find her along the creek bed, but as the days went by and there was still no sign of her, it became clear that someone had abducted her.

Among the townspeople assisting with the search was twenty-four-year-old Jack Spillman. Spillman had dated Dana Davis off and on over the past two years and lived with the Davis family for a while. When Penny went missing, he was living about eight miles away. Although he had grown up in Tonasket, he had dropped out of high school in the ninth grade and was known to move around repeatedly, staying with whoever could lend him a room.

Police first noticed Spillman in the early morning hours on the night that Penny had gone missing. He was driving his big black Chevy pickup truck down Patterson Creek Road near the Davis's home. When asked what he was doing that night, he told police that he had heard Penny was missing and had been helping with the search.

Within a few days, Spillman had become police's prime suspect after they looked at his prior criminal record. Among his offenses were burglary, theft, assault, and malicious mischief convictions. However, what concerned detectives the most was his arrest for rape. Just one year earlier, Spillman and another local man offered a woman a ride home from a bar. Once they got her alone, his friend raped her while Spillman held her down. The woman escaped before Spillman had a chance to take his turn raping her and she reported the attack. Both men were arrested and charged, but she later dropped the charges.

Police questioned Spillman about his whereabouts when Penny went missing and he claimed he was at a house party. Detectives spoke to other attendees that confirmed he was indeed at the party, but had left for several hours around 5:00 P.M. When he returned, his clothes were covered with mud. Nothing about Spillman's story seemed to hold up, but they lacked any evidence to convict him and kept him under constant surveillance for several months.

Six months later in March 1995, two hikers alerted the Okanogan County Sheriff's Department when they found what they thought to be part of a human jawbone in McLaughlin Canyon, just twelve miles from where Penny Davis was last seen.

When detectives arrived at the remote location, they found a shallow grave. Buried just a foot below the ground was the body of a young girl. Though the level of decomposition kept the medical examiner from determining a cause of death, DNA evidence later confirmed it was the body of Penny Davis.

Her body had been eviscerated — she had been cut open from the vagina to the chest, revealing the organs inside. The body was posed nude inside the shallow grave with the legs spread. By analyzing insect activity around the body, they could tell that the grave they found her in was not the murder scene, nor her original resting place. She had been buried somewhere for at least two weeks before she was moved and re-buried in McLaughlin Canyon. They knew this because the jawbone had been found outside of the grave — the person moving the body was unaware it had fallen off. It would have taken at least two weeks of decomposition for the jawbone to have fallen away from the skull that easily.

Police had been watching Spillman in the months prior, but just before Penny's body had been found, he had moved two hours south to Wenatchee, Washington, in Douglas County. In a regrettable move, Okanogan County authorities did not alert Douglas County authorities that their prime suspect in an abduction, now murder, had moved into their county.

Jack Spillman

Police informed Dana Davis that out of over one hundred potential suspects, all had been eliminated except for Jack

Spillman. Although they had no evidence to convict him, he was their primary suspect. They also told her of his criminal past and his prior rape accusation, but she still stood by him:

> "Jack is the kind of person who will walk away from an argument. That's not the kind of person that would brutally kill somebody."

In Wenatchee, when Spillman heard the news of Penny's body being found, he flew into an insane rage. He broke into the apartment of a woman that he knew lived with a young daughter. He'd had his eye on them for a while. While the family wasn't home, he broke into their house, took the young daughter's pet hamster, and mutilated it with a butcher's knife from the kitchen. Then, with the bloody hamster in his hands, he spun around in a circle, squeezing the hamster and spraying its blood all over the walls. He then took the bloody butcher's knife, stabbed it into the head of a stuffed panda bear, and left the house.

Since Spillman had moved to Wenatchee, the local police received numerous reports of local women being taunted and terrorized. The reports ranged from obscene phone calls to attempted rape. On one occasion, a woman called police and couldn't stop shaking because she was so terrified. In the middle of the night, Spillman had knocked on her front door, then ran around to the back door and knocked again. He then ran to the sides of the house and knocked all over the outside walls while she was alone in the house. When she walked outside to the side of her house, Spillman attacked her. He finally ran away when she kicked him in the groin and tore off a piece of his clothing. As Spillman ran, he called her by name and yelled, "I'll be back!"

On another occasion, as he was working as a roofer, Spillman would sit on the roof watching young girls below. One homeowner that was having their home remodeled found the family cat dismembered inside the home in a similar fashion as the hamster. It was later discovered that Spillman was responsible for that carnage as well. However, he ultimately had sadistic plans for more than just animals.

———

Ever since his arrival in Wenatchee, Spillman had been watching someone specific. He had his eye on fourteen-year-old Amanda "Mandy" Huffman. Amanda lived with her mother, forty-eight-year-old Rita Huffman.

Spillman first encountered Rita at the Igloo Tavern in East Wenatchee. She was walking through the bar toward a payphone when Spillman grabbed her arm and they had a brief exchange of words. It's unclear what was said, but it was obvious that something had pissed him off. He stormed out of the bar immediately afterwards without finishing his beer.

In the days after, Spillman creepily drove through the Huffman's neighborhood in his truck, watching Rita and her daughter. He sat in the bleachers at Amanda's softball games as she practiced after school. He watched both of them methodically for months before he made his move.

———

On the evening of April 12, 1995, Rita's adult daughter, Angie Zimmerman, had tried several times to call her mother, but got no answer. The next morning she tried again, but there was still no answer. Angie drove to her mother's house in the late morning and tried the front door, but it was locked. There was no answer when she knocked. Knowing that her mother always kept the back sliding door unlocked, she entered the home from the back.

When Angie walked in through the rear of the house, she went to her mother's bedroom to see if she was still asleep. What she found was an unimaginable bloodbath. Amanda's body was sprawled out on the bed, nude with her legs spread. A baseball bat had been shoved sixteen inches into her vagina. Like Penny, she had been sliced from her vagina up to her chest. The skin surrounding her vagina had been cut off and placed on her face. On the bedside table was a woman's breast, not Amanda's. Another was on the chest of drawers.

Angie was in shock and found herself unable to breathe. Without looking for her mother, she ran from the house and into the street screaming in terror. Unsure of what had happened, neighbors immediately called the police.

When police arrived to the scene, it was unlike anything they had ever seen. Douglas County Sheriff Dan LaRoche later told the media.

> "There's evidence of sexual mutilation, but I don't know if there's been any sexual assault. This is worse than any case we've ever had. All I can say is that there was very violent trauma. There doesn't appear to be evidence of a struggle or forced entry, but our visual search has been real brief. We just don't want to contaminate any blood or hair fibers that might be at the scene."

The body of Amanda's mother, Rita Huffman, was sprawled on the couch in the living room. Her nightgown had been ripped off and she had been cut from her vagina up to her chest. Both of her breasts had been cut off and she had thirty-one stab wounds on her chest, arms, legs, neck, and back. The skin around her vagina had been removed and shoved into her mouth.

Rita still wore a broken wristwatch which had stopped at 11:35 P.M. The detectives assumed the watch had been broken defending the knife attack and stopped at that time.

It was later determined that the removal of the breasts and skin around their vaginas was done postmortem — after they were already dead. The killer had spent hours in the home with the bodies after death. Rita died from her massive stab wounds and Amanda had died from a blow to the side of her head.

———

At 2:00 A.M. that morning, before the bodies had been found, Jack Spillman had been parked near a dumpster in the parking lot of a VFW hall when a police car approached him. As the officer approached Spillman he raised his hands, but at the time the officer was unaware that a murder had occurred just around the corner. Suspecting that he may be a burglar, the officer questioned him and let him go.

The next day, when detectives realized Spillman had been so close to the murder scene just hours after it occurred, they immediately took notice. Returning to the dumpster, detectives found a kitchen knife wedged in the bottom. The knife was covered in blood that matched the victims; it also matched a set of knives from the kitchen of the Huffman home.

Police then spoke to a neighbor that saw a black truck which matched the description of Spillman's parked in the nearby elementary school parking lot around 11:00 P.M. on the evening of the murder. The parking lot was in clear view of the back sliding door of the Huffman's home.

Jack Spillman was put under twenty-four-hour surveillance for two weeks while detectives gathered more evidence. When police watched him put more items into a dumpster near his house, they confiscated the entire dumpster and brought it back to the Sheriff's Office. Inside, they found a bloody ski mask that matched the DNA of Rita and Amanda, as well as his own. The blood of both victims was located around the mouth of the mask. Police later learned that he had drunk their blood during his rampage.

Two weeks after the murders, Jack Spillman was arrested. Police searched his home and truck and learned that he had left the gloves and clothes he was wearing during the killings on the seat of his truck. He had worn surgical gowns over his clothes during the killings and taped the gowns to his gloves and socks in hopes that he wouldn't leave any hair, fibers, or trace evidence at the scene. Fibers from the surgical gowns found at his home, however, were matched to fibers found at the scene.

———

While incarcerated in Washington State Penitentiary at Walla Walla, Spillman boasted of his crimes and told his cell-mate Mark Miller horrifying details about the murders and his plans to become the "world's greatest serial killer."

Spillman had read of serial killers extensively and continued to read about them in the prison library. He told Miller of how he had taped the surgical gowns to his socks and gloves and said, in the future, he would shave his entire body as well so he wouldn't leave any trace evidence. He went on to explain that with future murders, he planned to remove the bed linens and burn them, or burn the whole house down if necessary.

He explained that he knocked his victims out with a baseball bat before violating and dismembering them. That explained the blunt force trauma to Amanda's skull that killed her. He told Miller that his ultimate sexual fantasy was to be anally sodomized by a large male while torturing and mutilating his young female victims. This fantasy was so intense for him that he claimed that he could bring himself to orgasm just thinking about it.

He also told of his fantasies of inserting objects into his victim's vaginas, cutting genitals and breasts, and drinking the blood of his victims, ultimately pulling out their heart during the attack and eating it.

Spillman told Miller that he thought of himself as a werewolf and that he wanted to build an elaborate labyrinth of underground caves to keep his victims alive and torture them at will.

He went on to explain that Penny Davis was not his intended target; he had wanted to abduct and kill her thirteen-year-old friend, but the girl was able to get away from him, so he took Penny instead. He threw her over his shoulder so as to not leave her footprints and eventually tied her to a tree. He was sexually aroused by torturing her, but when he stabbed her in the stomach, he was disappointed because she died almost immediately after. He went on to say that he had sex with her dead body, then placed her into Patterson Creek. When he realized she wouldn't sink, he buried her instead.

He added that he exhumed the body several times and had sex with it to fulfill his necrophiliac fantasies.

———

Spillman's trial had been set for August 1996 and prosecutors planned to seek the death penalty, but in order to avoid the death sentence, he pleaded guilty to three counts of aggravated murder, robbery, and burglary. In April 1996, Jack Spillman received a sentence of life in prison without the possibility of parole, plus an extra 116 years.

CHAPTER 9
THE BLACK WIDOW

"The Black Widow" has been used as a moniker for numerous female killers through the years. However, when Canadian police in the tiny town of New Glasgow, Nova Scotia, notified the public that a serious potential offender was living in their midst, they were referring to eighty-year-old Melissa Ann Shepard.

———

In 2012, Fred Weeks was in his late seventies and spending his twilight years in a small retirement community when Millie Ann Russell (aka: Melissa Ann Shepard) knocked on his door. His conversation with the white-haired, rosy-cheeked Melissa was short and simple. She lived three doors down, had heard that he was widowed and lonely, and knew he was the same. That's all it took. Fred was instantly smitten.

Fred had lost his longtime wife just the year before and was excited to be in love again. It only took a few days before he asked Melissa to marry him. Fred called a friend who was a Justice of the Peace and the couple had an informal civil union ceremony in his living room. Afterward, they headed out for a romantic honeymoon in Newfoundland.

As Fred drove the car toward Newfoundland, his head became clouded and he couldn't think straight. Their trip involved a ferry journey and Fred thought that maybe he could rest a bit while the ferry sailed toward Newfoundland. However, by the time the ferry docked he had trouble finding his keys, needed to be reminded how to start the car, and couldn't figure out how to put the car into gear. By the following day, he couldn't put on his own shoes and needed a wheelchair.

When the couple returned to Nova Scotia, they checked into a bed-and-breakfast and Fred spent the entire night vomiting. The next morning, he fell out of bed and hit the wood floor. He needed to be hospitalized. Doctors tested his blood and found that he had ingested benzodiazepine, a tranquilizer used to treat anxiety. Melissa had been putting the drug in his coffee.

Police looked into the background of seventy-eight-year-old Millie Ann Russell and realized that they already knew her by several different names. Melissa Ann Russell was born in 1935 and, through several marriages, was known by the surnames Shepard, Stewart, Friedrich, and now Weeks. With the exception of her first marriage to Russell Shepard, all subsequent marriages ended in diabolical manipulation or death.

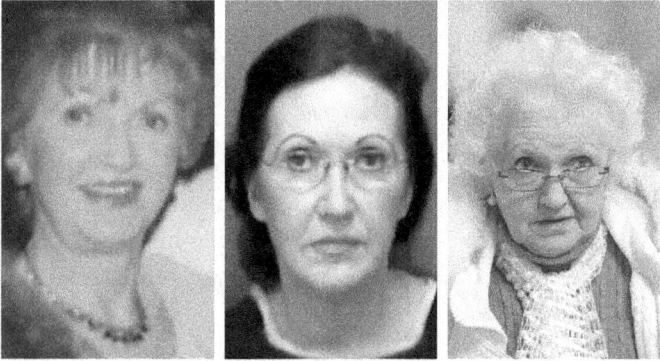

The many faces of Melissa Ann Shepard

Twenty-three years before meeting Fred Weeks in 1989, Melissa met forty-two-year-old Gordon Steward. Although his wife had died of cancer three years earlier, he was still grieving. Melissa was recently separated from her first husband and knew all the right things to say. Melissa and Gordon fell in love.

Gordon's family didn't think much of Melissa, though. After some digging, they realized that Melissa had been convicted of fraud more than thirty times using four different names and had served time in prison. However, Melissa convinced Gordon she had changed. That was the old Melissa. Although she wasn't yet divorced from her first husband, they flew to Las Vegas for a quick wedding and returned to Canada.

Almost immediately after the wedding, things started to fall apart. Suddenly Gordon was drinking more and more and their money supply was dwindling. When his drinking finally landed him in the hospital, doctors realized it wasn't just alcohol poisoning; there were drugs in his system, too.

In 1991, Melissa claimed that Gordon attacked her and threatened to rape her. He drove her out to a deserted logging road near Halifax. She told police that when he went behind the car to urinate, she stepped on the gas without realizing it was in reverse. She ran over her husband's head, then put it in drive and ran over him again before leaving the scene.

But her story had a huge hole. Gordon's toxicology report showed that he had enough drugs and alcohol in his system that he would have been unable to rape her, let alone drive a car. The level of drugs found in his system would have left him comatose; in fact, he would have died of an overdose had she not run over him.

Melissa was charged with the murder of her second husband, but only convicted of manslaughter and sentenced to six years in prison. Because of good behavior, she only served two of those years. The prosecution believed her motivation was monetary. After his death, Melissa was entitled to Gordon's pension.

When Melissa was paroled in 1994, she manipulated the public by passing herself off as a survivor of domestic abuse. Her new persona became a career for her and she was the focus of a documentary about abused women produced by the National Film Board, *When Women Kill*. She traveled throughout eastern Canada for speaking engagements, but the public eventually saw through her ruse. She knew it was time to start a new life, packed her bags, and headed for Florida.

———

Melissa met Robert Friedrich at a Florida Christian retreat in 2001. Like Gordon, Robert was grieving the loss of his wife of fifty-three years. Melissa believed that the Holy Spirit told her that he would be her next husband. Sure enough, just three days after meeting him, they were engaged to be married.

Robert's family protested the engagement, but he argued that he was getting older and didn't have much time left. Within a month they were married and set off on a five-month honeymoon, traveling throughout the United States. The honeymoon ended with an elaborate Caribbean cruise. By the time they returned to Robert's modest Florida trailer home, most of his $250,000 life savings had been depleted.

Within months of their return to Florida, Robert's sons living in Canada noticed a difference in their father. He began to have fainting spells and soon needed a walker. Several times he fell and required hospitalization. However, when his sons spoke to him on the phone and noticed his speech was often slurred, they grew suspicious and thought he was possibly being drugged.

The three brothers contacted an elder abuse agency in Florida that visited Robert and Melissa in their home. When the agency suggested that Robert should have twenty-four hour a day in-home nursing care or be admitted to a nursing home, Melissa flew into a rage.

She threatened to sue the elder abuse agency and left a rant on Robert's son's answering machine.

"Hello Bob, this is Melissa Friedrich calling. I have something to share with you this morning. Your father and I are going to see a lawyer. We've made an appointment. Your father is going to change his will. He's going to leave all the money to me except for the portion he had set aside for you and your two brothers. And that portion now is going to go to the Christian retreat. And you guys are getting nothing! A big fat zero! So try that on for size and have a nice day!"

In mid-December 2002, after just fourteen months of marriage, Robert mysteriously died of cardiac arrest. Melissa quickly had his body cremated and collected $100,000 in insurance money. She was also awarded his home, which she promptly sold. His family were left with a partial insurance policy.

Robert's family believed she had intentionally caused their father to overdose on a prescription drug that was not prescribed to him. Though they filed a criminal complaint against her, she was never charged with a crime in that case.

———

Despite her reputation in Nova Scotia, Melissa moved back to Canada in early 2004. However, by November of that year police realized that she had been receiving government funds and benefits using two different social insurance numbers. When police showed up to arrest her, she had already fled back to Florida.

Back in Florida, Melissa joined a dating website where she struck up a relationship with Alex Strategos. On their first face-to-face meeting, Alex and Melissa went to a nice romantic dinner. After coming back to his condo, Melissa didn't waste any time. They slept together that first night, but when he woke in the middle of the night to use the bathroom, his vision was blurry and he felt dizzy.

Over the next two months, Alex was hospitalized eight times. Like the men before him, Alex's family took notice of his quickly faltering health and his dwindling bank account. When he was admitted to the hospital and tests showed that he had tranquilizers in his system, Alex soon required a wheelchair and was admitted to a nursing home. The family knew she was poisoning him.

While he was in a drug-induced stupor, Melissa had him sign power of attorney over to her. She depleted his bank accounts and was in the process of selling his condo when his family alerted police.

Alex later said,

> "She's a nice woman, she treated me alright until she started giving me drugs."

Melissa was charged with forgery, grand theft, and using a forged document. She had been feeding him benzodiazepine in his ice cream. She pleaded guilty and was sentenced to five years in prison. After her prison sentence, she returned to Nova Scotia in 2012 using the name Millie Ann Russell.

———

This brings us back to the earlier story of her fourth husband, Fred Weeks, who she met by knocking on the door of his retirement home. Fred survived their fateful honeymoon trip to Newfoundland and Melissa was arrested yet again.

Police found an enormous amount of lorazepam, temazepam, and several other tranquilizer drugs in her belongings. The prescriptions were from five different doctors and she had used several different identities to obtain them.

Melissa was charged with attempted murder, but was only convicted of a lesser charge of "administering a noxious substance." She was released from prison at the age of eighty after serving only two years, nine months, and ten days. The conditions of her release were set: she was barred from using the Internet or any device capable of accessing the Internet, must report any relationship with a man and allow police to inform that man of her past, and she must allow police to photograph her if she changed her appearance.

Upon her release, police issued a press release advising citizens of Halifax that "a high risk offender is residing in our community."

Within a month of her release, Melissa Ann Shepard was arrested again for using a computer to access the Internet in a public library, violating the terms of her release.

CHAPTER 10
THE CROSSBOW KILLER

Scarborough is a large, beautiful area on the northern edges of Toronto, Canada. It was a suburb known for its diverse cultures and the stunning bluffs overlooking Lake Ontario.

Brett Ryan led a nice life in Scarborough, living with his parents and three brothers. In high school he was popular, athletic, and a hit with the girls with his spiked and gelled hair.

After graduating high school in 1997, Brett attended University of Toronto and did well academically. However, by his fourth year of college he had gone through two break-ups that hit him hard. His studies suffered and he dropped out in 2003, before he was able to graduate. After taking a year off from school, he re-enrolled in 2005, but again failed to graduate.

The next summer, Brett took a part-time job as a house painter while his friends graduated and got jobs in their fields. Though he had failed academically, he still planned for the future and did his best to be a credit to society. He volunteered his time with SickKids, a local charity, and coached Little League. By the end of summer, his part-time painting job had become full-time.

Despite having a shoestring budget with his painting job, Brett had extremely expensive taste. He liked to party with his friends, drove a nice car, and spent exorbitant amounts of money on trendy clothes. Versace, Dolce & Gabbana, Gucci, and Prada were his mainstays. He liked to live like he had money, but it was all borrowed. By his mid-twenties, Brett had over $60,000 in credit card debt and no savings to speak of.

It was all good, though: Brett had a plan. On the afternoon of October 20, 2007, twenty-six-year-old Brett Ryan walked into the Canadian International Bank of Commerce, not far from his home, with a bundle of papers in his hands. His arm was in a sling and his face was wrapped in hospital bandages. Without saying a word, he handed the teller a note. The note was concise and to the point:

> "Stay calm. Have gun. Withdraw $4,000, large bills. No, no games. 60 seconds. Go."

Though he only walked out the door with $1,115, it was exhilarating for him and he wanted more. A few weeks later, he robbed another bank. Then on Christmas Eve, another. He was hooked.

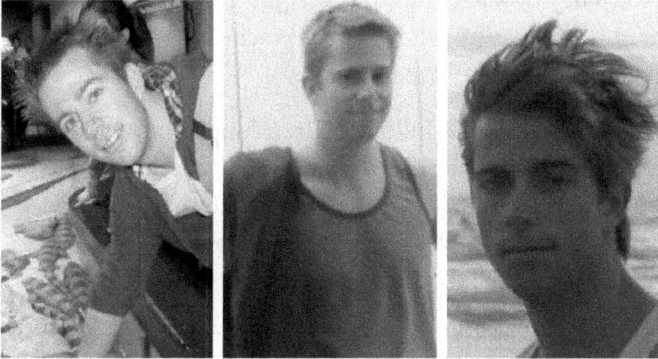

Brett Ryan

Knowing the police were looking for a man with an arm sling and bandages on his face, Brett decided to up his game. He posed as an old man with a very realistic long beard, glasses, and a Gilligan-style bucket hat. He walked with a limp. Again, he would simply hand the teller a note asking for a few thousand dollars and walk out of the bank with cash in his hand. The media dubbed him "The Bearded Bandit."

From October 2007 to June 2008, Brett made off with approximately $54,000, even robbing his own branch. Police were able to get a fingerprint off of one of the notes he passed to a teller, but Brett had never been arrested and his fingerprints weren't in any of the police databases.

At one point, police had twenty-five officers watching various local banks. Eventually police caught a break and spotted his truck leaving the scene of a robbery. Detectives followed Brett for two weeks before making a move on him.

On June 20, 2008, police knew who they were looking for and followed Brett from his home as he drove toward the bank. They watched the twenty-eight-year-old get into his car at his home, but when the car reached the bank, what appeared to be an old man exited.

Not knowing he was followed, Brett limped into the bank. As he approached the teller window, he paused for a second and turned around. Maybe he had second thoughts, or maybe he knew he was being followed, but police were waiting for him and he was arrested.

Brett pleaded guilty to all eight counts of robbery and an additional eight counts of using a disguise with intent to commit an indictable offense. He seemed genuinely remorseful for his crimes and was intent on turning his life around. Many of his family and friends wrote letters explaining to the judge that with this one exception, Brett had always been a good person and volunteered much of his time. With no prior police record, a sympathetic judge sentenced him to prison for three years and nine months.

Brett's mother, father, and three brothers rallied behind him, supporting him emotionally while he was in prison. While incarcerated, Brett was a model prisoner and was determined to get his life back on track. After only a year in prison, Brett was granted parole in April 2010.

Upon his release from prison, Brett moved back in with his family. They were forgiving and supporting; Brett was appreciative. His creditors, however, were not as supportive. The money he had stolen had not gone to paying his considerable debt and he filed for bankruptcy.

With his felony conviction, he had some trouble finding work. All it took was a quick google search of his name for a prospective employer to find out about his past. Even with his house-painting business, clients understandably didn't want him inside their homes. Eventually Brett got a job as a server at a downtown restaurant.

In the winter of 2010, Brett met Kristen Baxter on a blind date set up by a mutual friend. Kristen's life was very different from Brett's and everything he wanted his to be. She had a good job as a physiotherapist and owned a nice condo overlooking the waterfront. She enjoyed traveling and exercise.

Kristen knew that Brett had been the Bearded Bandit, but it didn't matter. They were in love and, by January 2013, he moved in with her in her high-rise condo.

For a brief time, life was bliss for the young couple and Brett proposed to Kristen with a small princess-cut diamond ring. She accepted. Brett had enrolled again at the University of Toronto and was actively looking for work in the technology field.

Brett & Kristen

A year after he moved in with Kristen, Brett's father died. Although Brett had had some trouble in his life, his mother Susan trusted him and made him executor of his father's estate. Brett spent much of his time over the following months with her. He performed tasks around the home and took care of the family finances, just as his father had done for years. Though his mother paid him for his work, his financial situation was still falling apart and, in 2015, one semester short of graduation, he dropped out of school again. This time, however, he didn't tell his fiancée or family. Instead, he told them he had graduated.

Brett still looked for work and things began looking up in the spring of 2016, when he was hired by a Toronto tech firm. Brett was finally on his way to earning a decent wage with a legitimate company. Kristen, Brett, and his family celebrated his new job and his recent graduation, but just days before he was to start work, his new employer googled his name. There was no way they were going to hire the Bearded Bandit. The tech firm let him go before he even started.

Brett was devastated and couldn't bring himself to tell Kristen, his mother, or his brothers. He went on with his life as if he had taken the job. Every morning he prepared for work, kissed Kristen goodbye, and got on the subway. In the evening he would arrive home to tell Kristen about his day at work, but it was all a lie. He had literally been riding the subway back and forth all day.

By that summer, Brett's stress mounted. Their wedding was just around the corner in mid-September. The ceremony was to be held at the Ancaster Mill, a bucolic event space along a bustling brook serving farm-to-table entrées at $100 a plate. Brett had a weekend bachelor party planned with friends at Mont Tremblant, a beautiful mountain resort town near Montreal. Kristen and Brett had also been looking at houses to buy, as the condo was a bit small for them. The obvious problem was that Brett's bank account was practically non-existent.

Susan Ryan was proud of her young son. As far as she knew, he had finally gotten a college degree, had a good job, and within a month would wed a beautiful, successful woman. She was more than happy to help with his finances, but when Brett finally told his mother the truth and asked for more money, the support turned to anger.

When Brett's mother learned that he had stacked lie upon lie for the past year, she was livid. Not only had he not told his family, but more importantly, he hadn't told the fiancée that he was planning to marry in less than a month. Brett's solution was to have his mother throw more money at the problem and hope it would all work out without having to tell Kristen. However, that just wasn't an option for Susan and she gave him an ultimatum. Either he told Kristen, or she would.

For Brett, his mother's option was no option at all. He had worked hard to gain the love of his perfect woman and he wasn't about to let his mother blow it.

Due to his felony conviction, Brett was not allowed to purchase a firearm. Instead, he purchased a second-hand Barnett Recruit Youth 30 Crossbow. The crossbow was small and light, designed for young hunters, but still strong enough to kill. Unlike a gun, a crossbow could easily be purchased without any kind of paper trail.

In the days after the argument with his mother, Brett continued to do remodeling work at her home. As he brought his construction equipment into the garage, he stashed the crossbow and arrows (bolts) in amongst the other items.

In the days prior to August 25, 2016, Brett had taken his time to note all of the security cameras in his building, as well as the cameras between his condo and his mother's house. It was all very similar to the preparation he had attempted to take back in his bank robber days.

Assuming he might make a mess, that morning Brett wore an extra set of clothes beneath his normal jeans and shirt, despite the summer heat and humidity. Inside a duffel bag he packed his Bearded Bandit disguise: the wig and bucket hat. Also inside the bag, he had packed a few extra crossbow bolts. Brett grabbed the bag and walked down the fourteen flights of stairs in his building to avoid security cameras.

When Brett arrived at his mother's house, he pleaded with her one last time to not tell Kristen that he hadn't graduated and didn't have a job. She refused and told him again that she would tell Kristen herself if he didn't. Susan then called Chris, Brett's oldest brother, and asked him to come help with the situation.

Brett fumed with anger and panic. He stomped out of the house and into the garage while his mother followed. A crossbow takes time to load and with his mother in hot pursuit behind him, he didn't have the time he thought he would. He grabbed one of the crossbow bolts and shoved the tip, with its three sharp blades, into her cheek. He then pulled it out and shoved it into her ear.

Susan was still alive, but bleeding profusely and struggling for her life. Brett threw his mother to the ground in the garage, grabbed a piece of yellow nylon rope, and strangled her to death.

Knowing that his brother Chris was on his way, Brett cocked the crossbow and inserted the bolt. Ready to fire, he waited quietly behind the side door of the garage. When Chris entered the garage, he didn't stand a chance. Without a sound, Brett placed the point of the crossbow bolt at the base of the back of his neck and pulled the trigger. The blades pierced the base of his skull and laid to rest in his mouth, killing him instantly.

Brett dragged Chris's body next to their mother's body and placed an orange construction tarp over them. His clothes were covered in blood, but he was prepared. He was about to remove his outer layer of clothing and put on his wig and hat when he heard his youngest brother drive up.

Brett walked out of the garage door with a crossbow bolt in his hand as A.J. walked up the driveway. Brett knew his plan had failed and he would need to kill them all. He met A.J. in the driveway and drove a crossbow bolt into his neck.

Brett's final remaining brother, Leigh, had been napping in the house and heard the screams. Looking out the window of the house, he could see his brother A.J. lying on the ground and Brett with a bloody crossbow bolt in his hand. Leigh picked up the phone to call 911, but Brett was having none of that.

Brett and Leigh fought inside the house, breaking furniture and spreading blood throughout the house. Leigh was able to get the bolt away from him, but was hit in the head in the process. Eventually Leigh made it out of the front door of the house and saw that his brother A.J., lying in the driveway, was still alive. Before Brett was able to catch him, Leigh ran to a neighbor's house and screamed for them to call the police. He made a point to tell the neighbor repeatedly to have the police come, not just an ambulance.

Brett realized there was nowhere to run. Out of breath and covered in blood, he calmly grabbed a bottle of water from the refrigerator, sat down on the front steps, and waited for police to arrive.

Though A.J. was still alive in the driveway at the time, he only lasted a few minutes longer and was dead by the time paramedics arrived. When the police pulled up, Brett told them,

> "The guys in the garage are dead. Crossbow to the head. It was me."

Worried that Kristen may have also been a victim of Brett's madness, Toronto police rushed to their waterfront condo. Though Kristen wasn't there, police were a bit startled and confused at what they found. Unsure what the items in their condo were, police evacuated the building and called in the bomb squad.

Inside the condo, they found Brett's MacBook Pro wedged against the wall with dumbbell weights. The screensaver had been turned off so the computer wouldn't go to sleep and the browser was open to YouTube. The cursor was hovering over the "play" button. Next to the computer was an oscillating fan set up with a digital timer. Duct-taped to the fan was a wooden spoon placed next to the "enter" key. The elaborate setup was just an alibi for Brett. When the timer went off, the oscillating fan would start and the spoon would hit the "enter" key, causing the YouTube video to play. Brett could have then said he was home watching YouTube videos when the murders occurred.

Two similar contraptions were set up with two additional oscillating fans and digital timers, one with an iPad and another with an iPhone. Each of those were set to send pre-written emails to friends at different times during the day. All this was for the purpose of establishing multiple digital fingerprints that he could later use as an alibi.

Though Brett went through all the trouble of configuring the elaborate alibi, he hadn't set the timers. He later explained that he had had a change of heart that morning and hadn't planned on killing his mother or brothers.

Brett Ryan pleaded guilty to second-degree murder of his mother, claiming that the crossbow was only to threaten her — not kill her. Because he had waited in the garage for his brother Chris to enter and killed him from behind, Brett pleaded guilty to the first-degree murder of Chris. In the case of the death of A.J., however, he had not expected him to show up and pleaded guilty to second-degree murder. He was convicted on all three counts, plus the attempted murder of his brother Leigh.

Brett received three concurrent life sentences for the lives he took, plus another concurrent ten-year sentence for the attempted murder conviction. He is eligible for parole in twenty-five years.

CHAPTER 11
MURDER IN THE SACRISTY

Even as a little girl, Margaret Ann Pahl knew she wanted to be a nun. When she told her parents of her plans, they weren't surprised. After all, two of her aunts had been nuns. Margaret Ann felt it was her life's destiny.

Sister Margaret Ann spent her life as a nun and was seventy-one years old in 1980 when she was working at Mercy Hospital in Toledo, Ohio. Although she had trained as a Registered Nurse, her hearing was failing and she was nearing retirement. She worked as the caretaker in the Hospital Chapel. It was Holy Saturday, the day before Easter, which coincidentally fell on her seventy-second birthday that year. Sister Margaret Ann woke early that morning, had a quick breakfast, and went to the chapel to prepare the Eucharist for Sunday's Easter services.

On what should have been a happy day for her, Sister Margaret Ann was in a foul mood that morning. She was very particular about how she felt the religious services were to be conducted at the Chapel and she wasn't happy with

Father Robinson's Good Friday service the day before. As she ate her breakfast, she told other chapel workers that she intended to speak to the Roman Catholic priest that day about how she felt about his sermon.

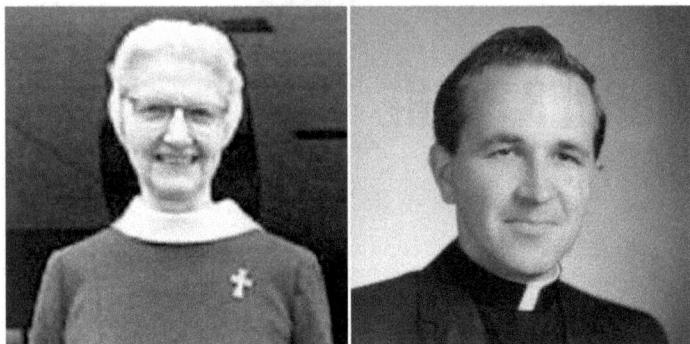

Sister Margaret Ann Pahl & Father Gerald Robinson

At 8:00 A.M. that morning, a young nun working in the hospital walked through the chapel and noticed a small folded cloth on the floor near the alter. It was strangely out of place. When she unfolded the cloth, she noticed that it was stained red with what seemed to be blood. At first she assumed someone had a cut themselves or had a bloody nose, but the stain itself had an odd shape. The nun set the cloth on a pew and walked into the nearby sacristy.

The nun immediately noticed that the polished gray marble floor of the small room was red with pooled blood. The motionless body of Sister Margaret Ann laid in the middle of the pool. Her clothes had been partially torn open and her legs were spread. An alter cloth filled with puncture holes and stains of blood had been draped over the body. In shock, the young nun screamed as she ran from the chapel to alert authorities.

Police arrived and found the sacristy, a small room just off of the alter where a priest would normally prepare for service, was filled with several gold chalices and crucifixes. Sister Margaret Ann's purse was also in the room, untouched. Robbery was clearly not a motive. When they removed the alter cloth, Sister Margaret Ann's body had thirty-one stab wounds in her neck and torso. Nine of the stab wounds on her chest formed an upside-down cross, as if the killing was some sort of ritual. Her forehead had been anointed with a smudge of blood - an obvious mockery of the Last Rites of the Roman Catholic Church. Her arms had been folded across her chest and the body was surrounded by lit candles. Everything about the scene seemed ritualistic.

An examination of the body showed that Sister Margaret Ann had been stabbed with a long, thin knife of some sort, like a tiny sword. From the indentations in her bones, they could tell the knife had a diamond-shaped tip. The stab wounds, however, were postmortem. Though her body was filled with holes, the official cause of death was strangulation. She had been choked to death, the alter cloth placed over her body, then stabbed repeatedly through the alter cloth after she had died. Stains on the alter cloth and bloody marks on the marble floor gave hints as to the shape of the weapon that was used.

Police examined the small folded cloth that the young nun had found earlier near the alter. When they unfolded it, they noticed a smudge of blood that resembled the smudge found on Sister Margaret Ann's forehead.

The community was shocked at the randomness of the murder and the ritualistic implications. For months, hospital staff were scared to walk the halls alone and raised money for a reward for the capture of the killer. Local authorities also wanted the killer captured and the Lucas county government offered an additional $10,000 in reward money.

Detectives and the forensic team spent weeks at the hospital processing the crime scene and questioning staff. Among the people questioned was Father Gerald Robinson, the Jesuit chaplain at the chapel that had presided over Sister Margaret Ann's funeral just four days after her death. Another chaplain at the hospital had accused him of the murder without actual proof.

Forty-year-old Father Robinson was well-liked at the hospital and had spent years preaching to sick and terminally ill patients. Two weeks after the murder, detectives searched his apartment and found a small sword-shaped letter opener with a diamond pointed tip. It was a souvenir from the United States Capitol and had a round medallion on the top in the shape of the capitol building, about the size of a dime. Detectives immediately thought it could have been the murder weapon and placed it into evidence.

Deputy Police Chief Ray Vetter was a devout Roman Catholic and familiar with Father Gerald Robinson. When Vetter found out that detectives were questioning a respected priest, he stopped the interview immediately and instructed the detectives to hand over all existing reports to him regarding the case. Reluctantly, detectives handed over their reports, several of which were never seen again. Chief Vetter told the detectives:

> "It was probably some screwball off the street. She just happened to be at the wrong place at the wrong time."

The prosecutor's office and the detectives working the case made accusations that there was a cover-up involved, but with the Chief of Police against them, the case was eventually dropped for lack of evidence. Six years later Chief Vetter had retired, but by then the case had slipped through the cracks. It had gone cold – and it stayed that way for more than two decades.

Father Robinson worked at the hospital for another year after Sister Margaret Ann's death until he was appointed to be the pastor at three parishes in suburban Toledo. In the mid-nineties, he became chaplain at Flower Hospital and the Lake Park Nursing Home.

———

Twenty-three years after the murder of Sister Margaret Ann Pahl, the Toledo Diocese received several accusations from both grown women and men that claimed they were sexually abused as children by a number of priests in the Diocese. Although the accusations were all horrific, one in particular was especially disturbing and involved Father Gerald Robinson.

In 2003, a woman in her forties came forward with a story that was hard to believe. She claimed that as a child, she was forced to be part of "Satanic ceremonies" performed by several Toledo Roman Catholic priests. She told authorities that the priests had placed her in a coffin filled with cockroaches, forced her to eat what she believed to be human eyeballs, and let a live snake penetrate her. The priests told her it was "to consecrate these orifices to Satan."

She also told police that the priests had killed a three-year-old child, performed an abortion on her, and mutilated dogs in Satanic sacrifices. When the woman made these claims, she had no idea that Father Robinson had been a suspect in a murder investigation two decades earlier.

Three other people came forward with disturbingly similar stories of abuse by Toledo Roman Catholic priests. Some of the accusers were too young at the time of their abuse to recall all the details, but all of them said the abuse came from many priests — one they were sure of was Father Gerald Robinson.

The news of the alleged abuse reached the Toledo prosecutor's office and detectives realized Father Robinson was involved. This news prompted the case of Sister Margaret Ann's murder to be pulled from the files and a cold case unit was assigned. They were going to give the entire case a new look, from top to bottom.

About seventy police reports that were earlier buried by the former Chief of Police were recovered and analyzed. One particular piece of evidence that was researched was the smudge mark on Sister Margaret Ann's forehead and the blood mark on the small cloth left near the chapel altar. Using new forensic technology that hadn't been available at the time of the murder, the blood stains from the cloth and her forehead were matched to the U.S. Capitol medallion at the top of Father Robinson's letter opener. Another blood stain on the ten-foot long alter cloth was matched to the ribbed handle on the letter opener. To obtain additional evidence, the body of Sister Margaret Ann was exhumed.

In April 2004, twenty-four years after the killing, Father Gerald Robinson was arrested for the murder of Sister Margaret Ann Pahl. During his interrogation, he told investigators he was innocent. He said he had been shocked when the nun was killed in his chapel and shocked again when the other chaplain had accused him of the murder.

At Father Robinson's trial, the prosecution produced three witnesses that had seen him near the chapel at the time of the killing. In addition to presenting the evidence of the imprint of the U.S. Capitol emblem on the cloth and her forehead, a medical examiner specializing in blood stain evidence testified that eighteen of the additional blood stains could have come from the letter opener. Photos of the stains were shown to jurors so they could see how closely it resembled the U.S. Capitol medallion. The prosecution was also able to provide evidence that the tip of the letter opener was a perfect fit for an indentation in her jawbone.

A Catholic priest that was an expert on the occult testified that the killing must have been committed by someone with a deep understanding of Catholic symbols and church rituals.

The prosecution argued that Father Robinson had tried to humiliate Sister Margaret Ann in death by stabbing an upside down cross into her chest and anointing her with her own blood in a ritualistic killing. Prosecutors said Father Robinson had been angry about Sister Pahl's domineering personality and her complaints about how he had conducted a Good Friday service the night before the killing.

Father Robinson maintained his innocence and wore his priest's collar throughout the entire trial. His defense team tried to argue that not all the DNA at the scene linked to him. They proposed a theory that Anthony and Nathaniel Cook, a pair of serial killer brothers that had been in the area at the time, could have committed the murder. There was, however, no evidence to support that theory.

———

On April 24, 2006, after nine days of testimony, Father Robinson was convicted on all accounts. The conviction represented the first documented time in history that a Catholic priest had killed a nun, as well as the second conviction of a Catholic priest for murder. Immediately upon his conviction, the judge sentenced him to fifteen-years to life behind bars.

In prison, sixty-eight-year-old Robinson remained a priest, but was barred from ministry. He filed multiple applications for appeal, but all of them were denied. In May 2014, he suffered a heart attack while in prison and died in July of the same year.

Despite his conviction and multiple accusations of ritualistic abuse, many of Robinson's lifelong parishioners stood by him, refusing to believe in his guilt.

CHAPTER 12
DEVIOUS DIXIE

Halloween 1984 was like any other Halloween for most people, but not for thirty-year-old Mel Dyson. He was working late at the office of the accounting firm that he worked for in Huntington Beach, California. His career as a financial consultant had paid off well. He worked hard and had nice cars and a nice three-story condo in an upscale complex in the Huntington Harbor marina. Life was good.

Mel's wife Dixie Dyson, however, worked in Los Angeles doing data entry. Although it was only twenty-five miles away, the L.A. traffic made it too much to commute on a daily basis. She and their seven-year-old son stayed at Mel's mother's house in Carson during the week and went to their Huntington Beach condo on the weekends. However, that routine had only started recently. Mel and Dixie had been struggling with their relationship for the past few years. They had been on-again-off-again until recently, when they decided to rekindle.

They had been together for almost ten years and had one child together, but had never actually married. Although California has no common-law marriage rule, the couple considered themselves husband and wife and Dixie took his last name.

Mel and Dixie met when he was in his early twenties. Dixie was ten years older, but that didn't seem to matter. The two were an odd couple. Mel grew up as an only child in a tight-knit Filipino family. He was shy and quiet, whereas Dixie was a loud, brash, and stocky blonde with cropped hair. She grew up as an adopted child of a broken family and had been married and divorced twice before. However, despite their differences, they were inseparable. At least for the first four years.

The second four years of their relationship were rocky. Mel and Dixie broke up briefly and she took their son south to San Diego county. Those four years were like a Yo-Yo. Over and over, she moved back in with him, then moved out again. But in October 1984, the couple were trying to patch things up.

————

When Mel Dyson finally arrived home that Halloween night, he was shocked to find that his beautiful condo had been trashed. Although the condo was in a secure complex with only one entrance that required going through a manned security guard station, someone had obviously been in the condo. Drawers were ripped from dressers, clothes thrown all over the house, artwork removed from the walls, and furniture overturned. Two of his watches had been stolen, his checkbook was missing, and about $300 in cash was gone.

When police arrived, they found no sign of forced entry and the guard at the gate had no record of any unauthorized person entering the complex. A window screen on the third floor had been torn, but a third-floor window hardly seemed a likely entry point. A burglar would have needed a very large ladder to get to that window, not to mention they would have had to come through the guard gate. None of it made sense.

———

On Saturday November 17, less than three weeks after the break-in, Dixie spent the day running errands and getting her hair done at the hairdresser. On her way back to the condo, she picked up their seven-year-old nephew who had planned to have a sleep-over with their son at the condo that night. That evening after the two boys were put to bed, Mel and Dixie went to bed and made love just after 10:00 P.M.

Sometime during the night, Dixie woke up to the sound of her son coughing and walked into his room to check on him. She found the two boys sound asleep, curled up next to her son, and slept for a while.

When Dixie woke up again later to go back to bed with Mel, she walked into the master bedroom and was immediately attacked. A man wearing a nylon stocking over his head held a knife to her throat, threw her to the ground, and raped her. Though the attack happened in the master bedroom, she didn't see her husband.

After the attacker finished with her, he forced her downstairs into the garage and gave her orders to get in her car and drive him out of the condo complex. She followed his instructions and drove him inland to the intersection of

Golden West Street and Warner Avenue, a busy shopping corner with strip-malls on all four corners. The rapist then exited the vehicle and ran away on foot, but before he left, he told her, "The last time was just a warning."

In a daze at what had just happened, Dixie drove back home to the condo. When she went back into the master bedroom, she noticed something she hadn't noticed while she was being raped. The entire bedroom was covered in blood and Mel was dead on the floor. His torso was a mesh of gaping stab wounds. Dixie rushed to check on the children and found them still asleep, unaware that anything had happened during the night.

When police arrived and Dixie told her story, they were instantly suspicious. She was cold and calm. She didn't act like someone who had just been raped and had her husband brutally murdered.

So many things about her story didn't add up. Dixie claimed the masked man raped her on the bedroom floor just a few feet from Mel's body. The room was covered in blood and the killer would have been covered in blood, but Dixie had no blood on her at all. In fact, while being raped, she didn't notice that Mel had been killed just a few feet away. When she was examined at the hospital, there was evidence that she'd had sex, but no evidence of violence or sexual trauma.

Like Halloween night, the only possible point of entry was the third-floor window. Again, a very unlikely scenario - but the most concerning fact was that the night guard working at the condo guard station had a completely different story to tell.

Dixie had told the police that she had driven the killer out of the complex at around 2:00 A.M., but the night guard logged the Dyson car leaving the complex at 1:30 A.M. Thirty minutes before she claimed and with only one person in the car, not two.

The guard also said that at 2:40 A.M., just twenty minutes before police arrived, a man of about forty-five and who called himself Carl drove up to the security gate with a woman that looked to be about thirty-five. They told the guard they were there to visit the Dyson family. The guard had called the Dyson home, spoke to a woman that answered, and gave them permission to enter. Dixie had no answer for any of this, claiming that the night guard must have been mistaken.

Dixie Dyson was immediately considered the prime suspect in her husband's death; their suspicions were magnified when she submitted claims on several life insurance policies that Mel had. She was due to receive approximately $140,000 in benefits.

In the months following the murder, police backtracked Dixie's movements over the prior years in an attempt to find evidence and build a case against her.

———

The last four years of Dixie and Mel's relationship had been tumultuous. They clashed almost constantly and for much of the time, Dixie had lived in San Diego county. During her time there, she had a relationship with a man named Enrico Vasquez.

Enrico was thirteen years younger than Dixie, but he was handsome and she was attracted to his bad-boy lifestyle. He grew up in rough neighborhoods of the Bronx, New York, and was a former Marine. Dixie fell for him hard. While she spent time away from Mel, she would use Mel's money to buy Enrico presents and spoil him at any chance she got.

A year after the murder, police received an anonymous call. According to the caller, Dixie Dyson had asked him to murder her husband. He told the police that she offered to pay him $10,000 once she received the life insurance money from Mel's death. The man said that he refused her offer, but knew that she had found someone else to do the job — her boyfriend, Enrico Vasquez.

Police believed that Dixie may have conspired with Enrico to kill her husband, but they had one problem with that theory. When shown a photo of Enrico, the night guard was absolutely certain that he was not the man that drove into the condo complex that night claiming to be "Carl." With a search warrant, police initiated surveillance of Dixie Dyson. All of her incoming and outgoing telephone calls were monitored and recorded.

In March 1986, using the federal search warrant, police intercepted a letter that she sent to New York City addressed to "E. Vasquez." In the letter Dixie said that an unidentified woman had offered to lend her money if she confessed:

> "She said I could have the money as long as I admitted to being involved in Mel's accident. Either I did it or know who did it, or arranged it. She said then her people would have some guarantee that I'd pay the money back or they could go to the police.
>
> Let me tell you, I was tempted. But I got scared and said no. I couldn't lie about it. She really started pushing it. I could have $15,000, $50,000 or whatever I wanted as long as I confessed to something."

Dixie went on to say that someone named "Mike" told her to stay away from the woman — that it was a setup.

> "With the circumstantial evidence, if I admitted anything to anyone they could pick me up. Although he [Mike] did say it was entrapment and he thinks a jury would laugh them out of town. But he says they definitely don't have enough to arrest me or they would have.
>
> There's never a day that goes by that I don't think of you. I get mad at myself that you are still so much a part of my thoughts.
>
> My God babe, can't you see how hard this is on me? I've got to get out. I think now is the best time. They think I'm stuck here, they won't be expecting it. Once I get the money, I think they'll really be watching to see what I do with it.
>
> Isn't there anyone you know that can help me? Don't you have any connections with the mob or loan sharks or anyone? I just can't take any more of this mental and emotional pressure. Knowing they [the police] are out there, that they still want me. It's never going to end for me as long as they know where I am.
>
> Please please, please help me. I need you now more than ever. Find three people to loan you $5,000. Please!!! Take care and don't get careless. They [the police] are still out there."

———

Two years had gone by since Mel Dyson's murder and there had still been no arrests in the case. Dixie Dyson had placed claims on Mel's life insurance policies, but all three insurance companies had denied them. They weren't in dispute of whether there was payment due, but rather they disputed who the beneficiary was.

Mel's mother, Delores, was the executor of his estate and had alerted the insurance companies that Dixie may have been involved in her son's death. After speaking to the police, the insurance companies agreed.

Claiming that the police had maliciously persuaded the insurance companies, Dixie hired a lawyer and planned to sue Allstate Life Insurance, Prudential Life, Security Life Insurance, the City of Huntington Beach, and Detective Mason, the lead investigator on her case. She was suing for the original $140,000 in life insurance, plus another $250,000 in damages. The court case was due to begin December 3, 1986, but the day before the case was to begin, Dixie was arrested for first-degree murder and conspiracy to commit murder.

———

Knowing that Dixie had visited the hair salon on the day of Mel's murder, detectives paid a visit to her hairdresser. At first her hairdresser was reluctant to talk, but eventually she told detectives that Enrico Vasquez called the salon the day of the murder and spoke to Dixie. Phone records confirmed the call.

The second piece of crucial evidence in the case was a drug store receipt found in Dixie's purse on the night of the murder. The receipt was from a store on the corner of Golden West Street and Warner Avenue — the very same intersection that Dixie claimed she had taken the killer. The timestamp on the receipt placed Dixie at the very same intersection just hours before Mel's death.

Another receipt found at the scene showed that Dixie had paid for flowers sent to Vasquez just weeks before the murder with a message, "Is it too late to start over?"

Though police knew that Dixie wasn't the actual killer and that Enrico Vasquez was involved, there still wasn't a warrant out for his arrest. Dixie's arrest report only listed that there was an "uncharged co-conspirator" involved. Detectives announced that, "This murder is still very much under investigation."

————

In March 1988, Dixie Dyson stood trial for the murder of her husband. Although most of the evidence against her was circumstantial, none of her excuses made sense.

Using the drug store receipt, the prosecution placed her at the same intersection where she claimed to have dropped off the killer just hours before the death. They proved that she didn't call the police until more than two hours after he was killed. She couldn't explain the lack of forced entry, nor the fact that she had no blood on her despite being raped on the bloody bedroom floor. They also placed motive on Dixie by showing how hard she had fought for the insurance money after Mel's death.

The defense attacked her dead husband. They argued that Mel may have been embezzling from his employer. More than $8,000 had gone missing at his work in the months before his death and the company was now facing bankruptcy. They argued that the police should have investigated the angle that someone from his company may have ordered a hit on him. Dixie also claimed that Mel was both verbally and physically abusive to her.

The key witness for the prosecution was the condo night security man. He had carefully logged every car that came through the gate on the evening of the murder and none of Dixie's explanations seemed to fit.

The jury deliberated for only two hours before coming back with a guilty verdict. First-Degree murder and conspiracy.

The jury foreman told the media:

> "Too many things in her story just didn't make sense. We just thought an innocent person would have done things a lot different from the way she did them."

> "We read that letter very carefully. There were just too many things in it that bothered us. She'd want him to call her at a phone booth instead of at home. If you're innocent, what would you care if the police overheard your conversation?"

Dixie faced an automatic twenty-five years to life, but before her official sentencing, she asked for a delay. She was ready to give up her accomplices. Without her attorney present, Dixie spoke to Dale Mason, the lead detective on the case. She knew that cooperation was her only chance of a lighter sentence.

Dixie told detectives that she had only planned the murder and asked her boyfriend Enrico to do the job for her. She told Enrico that with Mel gone, she would own the house, would have sole custody of her son, and would inherit $140,000 in life insurance.

Enrico wouldn't do it himself, but had a friend from New York City that would do it for a fee, George Ira Lamb. Days before the murder, Lamb had flown out from New York City and shared a nearby hotel room with Enrico Vasquez.

Dixie claimed that just hours before the attack, she met with Enrico and Lamb at a drug store on Golden West Street and Warner Avenue. From there, Lamb rode in the trunk of her car with her to the condo so the guard wouldn't see him on the way in. He stayed in the trunk until just after midnight, when Dixie went downstairs and turned on the garage light. That was his signal that he could get out of the trunk and come upstairs to kill Mel.

Dixie then watched as he murdered her husband. Afterward, they had consensual sex so that it would seem as though she was raped. After the murder, he climbed back into the trunk and Dixie drove him back to the same intersection.

To verify Dixie's story, police searched the trunk of her car. On the inside of the trunk they found a fingerprint that didn't belong to Mel, Dixie, or Enrico; they needed to find George Ira Lamb.

With the help of New York City police, Enrico and Lamb were tracked down and arrested in New York in the summer of 1988. Both were charged with first-degree murder and conspiracy and extradited to California for separate trials.

Dixie agreed to testify against both of her accomplices in exchange for a lighter sentence. Her twenty-five to life sentence was reduced to fifteen years to life.

———

During the three-week trial of George Lamb, Dixie told her story of how she and Enrico hired him to kill her husband. But Dixie had told stories before… most of them lies. The jury was having a hard time believing her.

Lamb's lawyers argued that seventeen stab wounds on a victim indicates a deep rage and hatred — not the work of someone that doesn't know the victim personally and just wants to get the job done.

Lamb's young wife and two-year-old son flew out for the trial, as did his great aunt, a New York State Legislator.

The jury deliberated for four days and came back with a not-guilty verdict for the crime of first-degree murder. For the charge of conspiracy, they delivered a guilty verdict. The jury believed that Dixie and Enrico had enlisted him to murder Mel, but he had changed his mind and didn't participate. They believed Lamb was involved, but Dixie's testimony could not be trusted.

Many members of the jury, however, didn't realize that the conspiracy conviction also came with a mandatory twenty-five to life sentence - the same as the murder charge. After the trial, five members of the jury took it upon themselves to petition the judge to allow Lamb leniency, saying they had no idea a conspiracy conviction held such a harsh penalty. The judge, however, denied their request, saying:

> "From what I see on the surface, Mr. Lamb is an upstanding young man. But this was a cold, calculated, first-degree murder straight up. They planned it, they got results."

———

Later that year, jurors at Enrico Vasquez's trial weren't so sympathetic. After seven days of deliberation, a jury convicted him of first-degree murder and conspiracy, which came with a mandatory twenty-five to life sentence.

In the end, Dixie Dyson was the mastermind behind her husband's death but, because of her cooperation with police, received a reduced sentence. Ultimately, however, she served a much longer sentence. In 2011, in a two-and-a-half hour deliberation, sixty-seven-year-old Dixie Dyson was denied parole.

CHAPTER 13
BONUS CHAPTER: THE BROOMSTICK KILLER

This chapter is a free bonus chapter from True Crime Case Histories: Volume 4

———

The tale of The Broomstick Killer is easily one of the most sinister stories in Texan history. Kenneth McDuff was a bloodthirsty killer who was granted unprecedented leniency by a justice system that allowed him to continue killing even after he had shown that he was a sadistic psychopath.

———

The tiny town of Rosebud in central Texas was the home of a notoriously strange family: the McDuffs. J.A. McDuff, the father, owned a cement finishing business that did quite well during the building boom of the late seventies, and the family was well-off by small town standards. The mother, Addie McDuff, ran the laundromat across from their home and doted over her six children. She was a large, headstrong woman known for being over-protective of her children, and would come running if they ever encountered trouble.

Addie was notoriously known to carry a gun in her purse and was referred to as the "Pistol-Packin' Mama" by the locals in Rosebud. Her children's teachers feared her because she would storm into the school in a huff any time one of her children was accused of misconduct. To Addie, her children could do no wrong whatsoever, and if someone accused them of anything, the school was likely to blame.

The eldest son, Lonnie, was the bully of the family. He once pulled a knife on the school principal who subsequently threw him down a flight of stairs. Lonnie spoke with a speech impediment and referred to himself as "Wuff and Tuff Wonnie McDuff."

Addie McDuff was particularly fond of her youngest son, Kenneth. Though technically he wasn't the youngest of the children, she fawned over him as her "baby boy." Even in his early teens when Kenneth started getting into trouble, somebody else was always to blame in her eyes.

Kenneth was a known troublemaker and a bully like his older brother Lonnie. He was always the kid with a pocketful of money, and new clothes, and he rode a loud motorcycle to school. Though he had an average IQ, he didn't do well in school. Kenneth didn't seem to care about school and his only genuine friend was his brother Lonnie.

By the fall of 1964 Kenneth was seventeen and spent most of his time causing trouble. He broke into businesses and homes looking for things to steal and drove around town looking for girls. But he wasn't looking for a girl to date: He was looking for a girl to rape. McDuff confided in his brother that he had once raped a woman, slit her throat, and left her dying. Whether the story was authentic is uncertain, as the crime was never reported.

Even at an early age, local law enforcement was all too familiar with Kenneth McDuff. Inevitably he was arrested in 1965 for a string of more than a dozen burglaries. The sentence for his crimes totaled fifty-two years, but because he was only eighteen the judge was lenient. McDuff was allowed to serve his time concurrently instead of consecutively. The fifty-two years of prison was reduced to a meager three years, and he only ended up serving ten months before they released him.

The brief sentence gave McDuff a sense of invincibility and just eight months later he moved on to much more heinous crimes.

On a hot August night in 1966, McDuff and his new friend Roy Dale Green were on their way to Fort Worth. Roy assumed they were on their way to drink some beer and look for girls, but McDuff had much more diabolical plans in mind.

Roy Dale Green was a skinny eighteen-year-old who was impressed with, and excited to be hanging out with twenty-year-old McDuff. Green knew that McDuff was a trouble-maker, but when Kenneth told him he wanted to rape a girl that night, Roy didn't take him seriously. When McDuff pulled into the parking lot of the baseball field in Everman, Texas, Roy had no idea what a mess he had got himself into.

McDuff pulled his car up next to a parked car near the baseball diamond; he could see there were three teenagers inside the car. He reached under the seat and pulled out a Colt .38 revolver, got out of the car, and walked up to the driver's side door of the parked car.

Pointing the revolver at the window, McDuff ordered the three teens out of the car. Inside the car was sixteen-year-old Edna Louise Sullivan, her boyfriend seventeen-year-old Robert Brand, and his fifteen-year-old cousin Mark Dunham. McDuff led them to the trunk of the car and commanded them to get in. The three teens climbed in, and he closed the lid.

Mark Dunham, Robert Brand & Edna Sullivan

McDuff drove their car while Roy Green followed in McDuff's car to an isolated area where they stopped. McDuff and Green got out of the cars and McDuff turned to Green and said, "We're gonna have to knock 'em off." Kenneth then opened the trunk and pulled Edna out. The teen girl screamed as he dragged her away from her friends to his own car and locked her in his trunk. He then went back over to the young boys. Unable to see, Edna's terror only intensified when she heard six gunshots. McDuff had emptied the revolver into the two other boys' bodies. When he could not close the trunk, McDuff became frustrated and backed the car up to a fence and abandoned it with the boy's bodies hanging out of the back.

Roy Green was in shock. They both got back in to McDuff's car and drove to another location where McDuff pulled Edna out of the back of the car and raped her. After he raped her, McDuff ordered Green to rape her too. Then McDuff yelled to Green, "Find something for me to strangle her with." Green pulled the belt off of his pants and handed it to him, but McDuff found something he liked better. He had a broom in the back of his car. He raped her with the broomstick, then sat on her chest and held it across her neck. He leaned forward on the broomstick, putting more and more pressure on her neck until he crushed her throat. McDuff threw her body over his shoulder, walked to the side of the dirt road and tossed her body into the nearby bushes; the two drove away.

The next day Roy Green was consumed with guilt and told his friend's mother what they had done. His friend's mother went to Green's mother, who subsequently convinced him to turn himself in.

Green was arrested and led the police to the bodies, and McDuff was quickly arrested as well. Green gave the police the gun that McDuff had buried next to his garage.

During the trial, a terrified Roy Green stuttered and stammered as he testified against McDuff. McDuff was cocky and nonchalant, taking the stand in his own defense, but it didn't help his case.

Kenneth McDuff mugshots

In November 1966 a jury found Kenneth McDuff guilty on three counts of murder. Roy Green served eleven years in prison for his part in the murders, while McDuff was handed three death sentences in the electric chair. In a normal world, this would be the end of the story, but it was nowhere near over.

On June 29, 1972 after six years on death row, the US Supreme Court decided that the death penalty, as it was then written, was a cruel and unusual punishment and was therefore unconstitutional under the Eighth and Fourteenth Amendments. In an extraordinary event, all death penalty cases in the United States were commuted to life sentences.

McDuff was now eligible for parole and applied for it every time he was allowed. He was convicted of such heinous crimes; it was unimaginable that he would ever be paroled. The residents of Central Texas thought that such a vicious killer could never be paroled. Over and over he applied, and he was repeatedly denied.

Fifteen years later in 1987, McDuff saw his chance. The Texas Federal Court ruled that the prisons of Texas were far too overcrowded, violating the civil rights of the inmates. Rather than spend money building more prisons, the courts set population limits in the prisons which led to a massive backlog of inmates being held in county jails across the state.

Texas Governor Bill Clements made an unthinkable deal with the parole board. In order to reduce prison population, they were required to release 150 inmates per day. Initially, the white-collar crimes were released, then the minor drug offenses. Within two years the only people left in the prisons were murderers. This is when McDuff saw his chance.

Each time he applied for parole, McDuff still had to appear before a parole board of three members, plead his case, and get two out of three votes in his favor. He had tried several times and was denied each time. In one instance he actually received two votes, but it was ultimately denied when an unknown party argued against his release. In another instance he tried to bribe a parole board official by offering him $10,000. Each time he was denied, but it didn't deter him.

Outside of the prison, McDuff's mother was busy doing her part. She hired two well-known attorneys from Huntsville, paying them $2,200 to try to find a way to get her beloved son released from prison.

Unbelievably, in 1989, after serving twenty-three years in prison, McDuff was paroled. The two members of the parole board that voted to release him were James Granberry and Chris Mealy. Mealy later blamed the tremendous pressure he was under from the government. Granberry was later charged with perjury in an unrelated case and ordered to serve six months in a halfway house.

During those years, the Texas parole board set free 127 murderers and twenty death row inmates.

———

The people of Rosebud were in shock at the news of McDuff's release. Some put bars over their windows and many feared walking the streets of the tiny town without a gun.

Immediately after his release, McDuff was required to visit his parole officer in Temple, Texas. After their first visit, the parole officer told police,

> "I don't know if it'll be next week or next month or next year, but one of these days, dead girls are gonna start turning up, and when that happens, the man you need to look for is Kenneth McDuff."

The parole officer was right. Just three days after his release, the body of twenty-nine-year-old Sarafia Parker was found in a field twenty-five miles west of Rosebud in Temple, the town that McDuff's parents had moved to while he was in prison. Though they had no evidence, police suspected McDuff was responsible for the killing.

McDuff was known as a racist. Just seven months after his release he harassed a young black man in Rosebud, yelling racial slurs at him, and pulled a knife on him. This violated his parole, and he was quickly sent back to prison, but McDuff knew how the prison system worked. He knew about the overcrowding issues and he was back on the streets just two months later.

After his release from prison, McDuff enrolled at Texas State Technical College in Waco and briefly got a job as a cashier at a convenience store called Quik-Pak. But working for a lowly $4 an hour did not satisfy him, and he quit after only a month.

By the summer of 1991, McDuff had given up his feeble attempts at the straight-and-narrow life and continued his life of crime. Living in the college dorms, he started dealing and using drugs. He knew this violated his parole, but he didn't care. He spent his spare time picking up prostitutes in Waco and used them to satisfy his need for violent sex.

In the late hours of October 10, 1991, McDuff picked up a young crack-addicted prostitute from Waco, Brenda Thompson, intent on killing her. McDuff had Brenda tied up in the passenger seat of his red pickup truck when he noticed a police checkpoint up ahead. Brenda saw her opportunity and screamed as she raised her legs up to the windshield and began kicking, cracking the windshield several times. When the police ran toward his truck McDuff hit the gas and crashed the roadblock. Several police officers had to jump out of the way to avoid being run over.

McDuff led police on a high-speed chase but escaped into the night by turning off his lights and driving the wrong way down one-way streets. After he escaped, he took Brenda Thompson down an old abandoned road into a wooded area near Route 84 where he raped, tortured, and murdered her. Her body wasn't found until seven years later.

Just a week later McDuff picked up another Waco prostitute. Seventeen-year-old Regina DeAnne Moore was last seen arguing outside a motel with McDuff on the night of October 17. Again, McDuff tied her arms and legs with her own stockings, then took her to a remote area where he raped and murdered her. Her remains were not found until 1998.

Two months later in Austin, twenty-eight-year-old Colleen Reed was washing her shiny new Mazda Miata convertible at a self-serve car wash.

One thing that McDuff learned in prison was to find a malleable sidekick. That evening he was driving around Austin with his latest sidekick, Alva Hank Worley. As they drove past the car wash McDuff spotted Colleen and made a quick U-turn.

McDuff pulled his tan Thunderbird into the bay next to hers, got out of the car and walked into Colleen's stall. Without a word, McDuff grabbed her around the neck and lifted the tiny girl off the ground. When Colleen screamed, neighbors behind the car wash came out to see what was happening. They watched as McDuff threw Colleen in his car and he and Worley drove away, again driving the wrong way on a one-way street.

The witnesses got a good look at Worley and alerted the police of his description and the type and color of the vehicle that sped away. Right away police suspected that McDuff was behind the abduction.

When police got the description of Worley, they began looking through McDuff's known associates and noticed Hank Worley immediately as one of his known drinking buddies. Like Roy Dale Green, Worley was timid and easily influenced by McDuff.

Worley wasn't hard to find, living in a motel with his four-teen-year-old daughter. When police knocked on his door, he was already terrified with guilt.

Though his guilt consumed him, he feared McDuff and wasn't quite ready to point a finger at him. On the first visit to his motel room, Worley claimed he barely knew McDuff. It took a few visits to his motel room for police to persuade him to admit to what had happened that night. They stopped by while he was having a barbecue by the motel pool with his daughter, and Detective Mike McNamara whispered in his ear,

> "Hank, you're hiding a kid killer, you know that? You're protecting a man who raped and brutalized and strangled a girl not much older than your daughter over there. Picture her on the ground, a broomstick across her throat, crying out for you to help, begging you to speak out, to do what's right, to save the life of some young girl, to…"

McNamara couldn't finish his sentence before Worley screamed. He was ready to talk. When investigators got him into the interrogation room, he told the complete story of the night of Colleen's abduction.

Worley said he and McDuff were in Austin looking for drugs when McDuff saw Colleen washing her car. When McDuff lifted her off the ground by her throat she screamed "Please, not me! Not me!" He then threw her in the back of their car and told Worley to hold her down as they sped off.

When they got a few miles out of Austin McDuff got in the back with Colleen and commanded Worley to keep driving out of town. McDuff tied her hands behind her back with her shoelaces, then took his cigarette and put it out between her legs as she screamed. He beat her and raped her. When he finished, he told Worley to change places with him and Worley raped her while McDuff drove.

> Worley recalled, "I didn't want to have sex with her but if I didn't have sex with her, I knew that he was gonna get back there with her and beat her up some more and burn her with cigarettes. He was taking the cigarettes and getting the fire real hot and burning her down there in the wrong spots."

When they got near the town of Belton, McDuff pulled onto a secluded dirt road and raped her again.

> "He turned around, and he hit her. Slapped her real hard and knocked her backwards. Then he took another cigarette, and he lit it, and got the fire real hot and he burned her like that again."

When she was able to stand Worley claimed Colleen put her head on his shoulder and said "Please don't let him hurt me anymore." McDuff was having none of that. He grabbed her by the neck and stuffed her into the trunk of the car and turned to Worley and said, "I'm gonna use her up." McDuff used the term often to mean that he was going to terminate her life.

> "Then he put her in the trunk of the car, closed the trunk down and he takes me home. On the way home he asked me for my pocketknife and I told him I don't know where it is."

> "Then he asked me, 'Well, I need a shovel. Let me borrow a shovel.' And I said, 'I ain't got one.' He didn't say what he was going to do with it, but I knew what he was gonna do with it. He wanted to kill her with it."

"Ain't nothin' I could do. Real scary being like that. If you can't help yourself, there ain't no way you gonna help anybody else. I wasn't even sure if I was gonna make it outta that."

"I'll always have a tear for that girl. I'll always cry for her, for what she went through. Nobody should be put through that type of torture."

McDuff was nowhere to be found, but police knew he was still in the area the following February when they found the body of another young prostitute. Twenty-two-year-old Valencia Joshua, a student at the same college that McDuff had attended was found on a golf course near the school. She had been strangled. The last time anyone had seen her, she was looking for Kenneth McDuff on the campus of their school.

Then on March 1, 1992, Melissa Northrup was working the night-shift at the Quik-Pak convenience store. She was a pregnant mother of two who knew the dangers of working the night shift, but needed to pay the bills. She would regularly call her husband during her shift to let him know she was okay.

Late that night McDuff was cruising the streets looking for drugs when his tan Thunderbird broke down just 100 yards from the Quik-Pak. This was the same store that McDuff had worked for only a month. McDuff knew that the store was open twenty-four hours a day and had no security to speak of. He also knew that there was a cute twenty-three-year-old who worked the night shift and had told friends that the place could easily be robbed.

When Melissa's husband didn't hear from her at 4:00 a.m. that night he got worried and called the store. He repeatedly got no answer so he drove to the store, but there was no sign of his wife.

When police found McDuff's car abandoned at the New Road Inn just 100 yards away, their suspicions were confirmed. McDuff was on a killing spree, and they started a massive nationwide manhunt.

Knowing how close McDuff was with his family, they started by questioning his parents. As always, his mother stood by her beloved son and claimed he was innocent but didn't know where he was. His father, however, was less loving,

> "I don't know where he is. If you find him, you can kill him if you want to."

On April 26, the badly decomposed body of Quik-Pak employee Melissa Northrup was found floating in a gravel quarry in Dallas County. Her hands were still tied behind her back with shoelaces - a signature of Kenneth McDuff.

The big break came on May 1 when the manhunt was aired on America's Most Wanted. The TV show was massively popular; through the years it has helped capture 1,200 fugitives. This airing was no exception. Shortly after it aired a man called from Kansas City, Missouri claiming that McDuff worked for a trash company under the assumed name Richard Fowler.

Texas police called Kansas City police who looked up the name Richard Fowler in their records. Someone had been using the name and had been arrested and fingerprinted for soliciting prostitutes. The fingerprints matched that of Kenneth McDuff. McDuff was arrested on May 4, 1992 as he was driving a trash truck to a landfill.

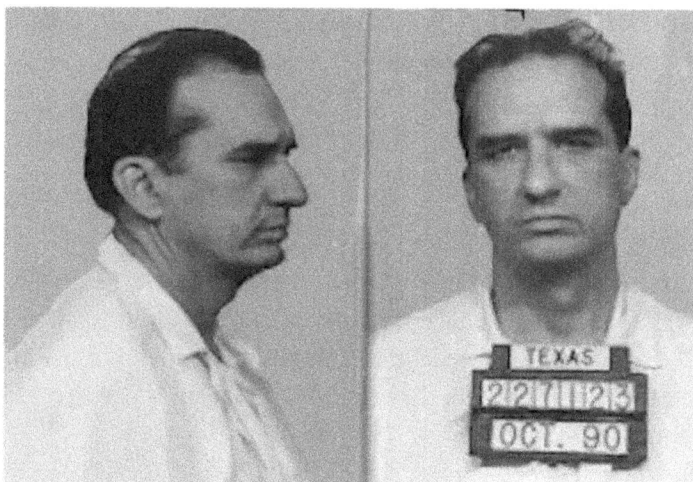

McDuff 1990 Mugshot

When he was brought back to Texas, crowds of angry people gathered outside of the courthouse. McDuff embraced the media and professed his innocence to the mob of cameras outside, often claiming that his trial was unfair.

Prosecutors had their strongest evidence against him for the abduction and murder of Melissa Northrup, so they decided to try that case first and worry about the rest later.

Addie McDuff, who was now seventy-seven years old, was called as a hostile witness to testify against her son. She confirmed that her son used her credit card near the Quik-Pak store on the night of the abduction, putting him near the scene of the crime when it happened.

McDuff was livid that his own mother was being used by the prosecution to testify against him, but there was more to come. The prosecution called two of his friends to testify that he had tried to enlist them in his plans to rob the Quik-Pak store.

At one point McDuff directed his anger at his own attorneys when he screamed at them,

> "Why don't you get up and go sit on the prosecution's side! You're helping them more than you are me!"

The murder of Colleen Reed had not been tried yet, and the prosecution called Hank Worley to testify to show that there was a signature to McDuff's killings. Worley was brought to the courthouse in handcuffs. From his visible shaking, it was clear that just being in the presence of McDuff again terrified him.

The ultimate nail in the coffin for McDuff was when he insisted on testifying on his own behalf despite his defense team's wishes. They explained to him that under the rules of evidence, his past 1966 murders couldn't be mentioned in court if he wasn't on the stand, but if he took the stand, the prosecution could use that against him. McDuff wouldn't listen.

McDuff took the stand for two hours rambling a nonsensical story of his whereabouts on the night of the murder. Meanwhile, the prosecution took advantage of their opportunity and the jury heard the complete story of his brutal killings of the teenagers in 1966.

The jury took four hours to return their guilty verdict on February 16, 1993. His defense team requested leniency and asked for a life sentence, but the jury only took one hour to decide that Kenneth McDuff should die by lethal injection.

McDuff's trial for the murder of Colleen Reed started in 1994. Although the body had still not been found, he was given a second death sentence.

In television interviews from prison awaiting his death sentence, McDuff continued to profess his innocence, even for the 1966 killings.

In the months before his execution, investigators enlisted the help of a jailhouse informant to try to get McDuff to give up the locations of the bodies. Their plan worked.

In September 1998, the body of Regina DeAnne Moore was found beneath a bridge on the side of a highway. McDuff had buried her in a shallow grave. Her hands were still tied behind her back with shoelaces, and her ankles were bound with stockings.

The body of Brenda Thompson, who kicked McDuff's windshield as he crashed through the roadblock, was found in a grouping of trees outside of Waco. She had been tied up, raped, and tortured.

McDuff only had two weeks before his execution, but he wasn't giving up the location of Colleen Reed. He told the informant that he didn't want to tell the cops because it was the last body and if he gave them everything they needed they would "take away my commissary rights, and won't treat me right." With only two weeks to live, McDuff's only concern was his own diminished rights and had no regard for the closure of his victim's families.

Police met with prison officials and arranged to take none of his prison rights away. Presented with the assurance, McDuff finally gave them directions to where he had buried Colleen Reed's body.

Despite digging for hours exactly where he told them, they were unable to locate her body. That afternoon, in a covert arrangement, McDuff was brought to the dig site. The body of Colleen Reed was found on October 6, 1998.

In McDuff's final days investigator John Moriarty spent over forty hours interviewing him, trying to gain a deeper understanding of the psychopath's mind. In the time he spent with him, though he showed no remorse at all, McDuff admitted to all eight murders and alluded that there may have been many more.

Kenneth McDuff was executed on November 17, 1998. His family didn't claim his body, and he was buried in in the Huntsville prison graveyard with a tombstone that displayed only his death row number X999055 and the day of execution.

As a result of the mayhem that McDuff caused and an outcry from the public, the Texas parole system was completely overhauled and the state spent $2 billion building more prisons.

———

This chapter is a free bonus chapter from True Crime Case Histories: Volume 4

Online Appendix

Visit my website for additional photos and videos pertaining to the cases in this book:

http://TrueCrimeCaseHistories.com/vol5/

More books by Jason Neal

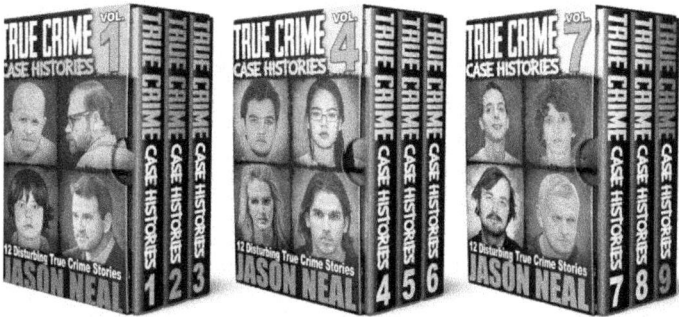

Looking for more?? I am constantly adding new volumes of True Crime Case Histories. The series **can be read in any order**, and all books are available in paperback, hardcover, and audiobook.

Check out the complete series at:

https://amazon.com/author/jason-neal

All Jason Neal books are also available in **AudioBook format at Audible.com.** Enjoy a **Free Audiobook** when you signup for a 30-Day trial using this link:

https://geni.us/AudibleTrueCrime

FREE BONUS EBOOK FOR MY READERS

As my way of saying "Thank you" for downloading, I'm giving away a FREE True Crime e-book I think you'll enjoy.

https://TrueCrimeCaseHistories.com

Just click the link above to let me know where to send your free book!

THANK YOU!

Thank you for reading this Volume of True Crime Case Histories. I truly hope you enjoyed it. If you did, I would be sincerely grateful if you would take a few minutes to write a review for me on Amazon using the link below.

https://geni.us/TrueCrime5

I'd also like to encourage you to sign-up for my email list for updates, discounts and freebies on future books! I promise I'll make it worth your while with future freebies.

http://truecrimecasehistories.com

And please take a moment and follow me on Amazon.

One last thing. As I mentioned previously, many of the stories in this series were suggested to me by readers like you. I like to feature stories that many true crime fans haven't heard of, so if there's a story that you remember from the past that you haven't seen covered by other true crime sources, please send me any details you can remember and I will do my best to research it. Or if you'd like to contact me for any other reason free to email me at:

jasonnealbooks@gmail.com

https://linktr.ee/JasonNeal

Thanks so much,

Jason Neal

ABOUT THE AUTHOR

Jason Neal is a Best-Selling American True Crime Author living in Hawaii with his Turkish-British wife. Jason started his writing career in the late eighties as a music industry publisher and wrote his first true crime collection in 2019.

As a boy growing up in the eighties just south of Seattle, Jason became interested in true crime stories after hearing the news of the Green River Killer so close to his home. Over the subsequent years he would read everything he could get his hands on about true crime and serial killers.

As he approached 50, Jason began to assemble stories of the crimes that have fascinated him most throughout his life. He's especially obsessed by cases solved by sheer luck, amazing police work, and groundbreaking technology like early DNA cases and more recently reverse genealogy.

🄖 BB ⓐ ♪ f